500

breakfast & brunch dishes

500

breakfast & brunch dishes

the only compendium of breakfast dishes you'll ever need

Carol Beckerman

SELLERS
PUBLISHING

A Quintet Book

Published by Sellers Publishing, Inc.
161 John Roberts Road, South Portland, Maine 04106
For ordering information:
(800) 625-3386 Toll Free
(207) 772-6814 Fax
Visit our Web site: www.sellerspublishing.com
E-mail: rsp@rsvp.com

ISBN: 978-1-4162-0620-0
Library of Congress Control Number: 2010932867
QTT.FHBB

This book was conceived, designed, and produced by
Quintet Publishing Limited
6 Blundell Street
London N7 9BH
United Kingdom

Food Stylists: Carol Beckerman, Valentina Sforza
Photographer: Ian Garlick
Art Director: Michael Charles
Editorial Assistants: Carly Beckerman-Boys, Holly Willsher
Managing Editor: Donna Gregory
Publisher: James Tavendale

10 9 8 7 6 5 4 3 2 1

Printed in China by 1010 Printing International Ltd.

contents

introduction

Eat breakfast...be happy! People often say they skip breakfast because they do not have time, or simply because they are not hungry. But cliché or not, breakfast is certainly the most important meal of the day. When you wake up in the morning, you will not have eaten for about twelve hours, so your body is like a car that has run out of gas. You need fuel, and you need it first thing in the morning if you want to get the most out of your day.

Without a doubt, breakfast provides the energy we need for daily life, boosting the metabolism and getting the body burning calories efficiently. It provides essential vitamins and nutrients, and it can also help you maintain your weight. There is some evidence to suggest that children and adults who eat breakfast regularly perform better and are less likely to be overweight than those who do not. Also, skipping breakfast is strongly linked to the development of obesity. Studies show that overweight and obese children, adolescents, and adults are less likely to eat breakfast than their slimmer counterparts.

The average working woman and man needs around 2,100 and 2,800 calories a day respectively, and if you are engaged in heavy physical work or exercise, you will need more. If you spread out your calorie intake sensibly over three meals per day, you should be thinking of eating a breakfast comprising around 800 or 1,000 calories.

While adults need breakfast, children need it even more. When they skip breakfast, they can end up going for as long as 18 hours without food from the evening meal to lunch the next

day, taking into account that an evening meal will probably be eaten around 6 p.m., and lunch the next day will not arrive until roughly noon. This period of semistarvation can create a lot of physical, intellectual, and behavioral problems. If you or your children regularly skip breakfast, remember that eating a wholesome, nutritious morning meal will probably save you time in the long run.

By recharging your brain and your body, you will be more efficient in just about everything that you do. Not eating breakfast tends to make you tired and lethargic, encourages you to eat more at your next meal, and can cause you to snack on high-calorie, less nutritious foods to stave off hunger.

One reason people give for skipping breakfast is that they do not know what to eat. This book will show you how diverse the possibilities are when considering your breakfast menu.

Whether you have breakfast in a leisurely fashion at home, on the run, or at work, you will find lots of ideas to build on. From romantic breakfasts in bed to brown-bagged breakfast sandwiches and brunches with family and friends, all the recipes are found here, in one easy-to-use book.

breakfasts from around the world

Adding to the diverse collection of dishes found in this book, there are many new flavor combinations and exciting recipes from around the world. Breakfasts tend to be very different depending on country and culture of origin.

In Poland, for example, a substantial platter is usually served for breakfast. This includes cold meats, meat pastes, polish sausage, sardines, tomatoes, and sliced pickles, eaten with an array of side dishes. In some countries, China for instance, the same food is eaten for breakfast, lunch, and dinner. Generally speaking, it is rice eaten with small amounts of vegetables and meat. In Japan, many people eat a Western-style breakfast—but traditionally breakfast would consist of steamed rice, miso soup, and various side dishes. Boiled or broiled fish, omelets, and dried seaweed might also be served.

In Malaysia, a popular breakfast is called *nasi lemek*, which is simply rice, cooked in coconut milk, with various extra ingredients tossed into the pot to add fragrance. It is available on just about every street corner and in almost every local restaurant, served with chicken or beef, and even cuttlefish. Malaysians also like *kaya*, a sort of jelly made with eggs, sugar, and coconut milk, which is spread on toast.

In Europe, you will find the countries that define the term "continental breakfast." These countries eat a large lunch, and the first meal of the day is the absolute minimum of stimulant and sustenance: coffee and bread. In France, the popular choice is café au lait, served in large ceramic bowls. The bread is usually a croissant, brioche, or a slice of toast, with butter and good-quality fruit preserves. Another popular choice is hot chocolate.

Germans like something a bit more substantial—a selection of freshly baked rolls, which will often be served with a generous selection of cold meats, cheeses, fruit, and yogurt. Bavarian sausages are popular, made from finely minced veal and fresh bacon.

Breakfast in Italy is generally sweet. Cake is a traditional Italian breakfast food, as are cookies. There is no tradition in Italy of savory food on the breakfast table, and hot coffee or cappuccino is served with pastries, brioche, croissants, or toast.

The Spanish like to have a light breakfast and a large lunch too. Here breakfast is the smallest meal of the day. They like sweet rolls called magdalenas, lemon cupcakes, and sugary, deep-fried churros with chocolate.

In Finland they eat a pancake called *panmi kakku*, which is made from batter using evaporated milk. In Slovakia, it would be salami and cheese, eaten with bread rolls and butter. Some people have mustard with it, some prefer onion.

Romanian cuisine is very diverse. It includes a lot of customs and culinary traditions, having been influenced along the way by other nationalities it has come into contact with. These would include the Turks, Hungarians, and Slavs. There is no traditional first meal of the day in Romania, so it varies from region to region. In the cities, people grab whatever is quick, whereas in the countryside, they eat something called *mamaliga*, a sort of cornmeal mush, served with cold milk. They also eat bread, dairy products, vegetables, tomatoes, onions, and eggs. A continental breakfast is now much more popular in Romania than it used to be.

The British love their traditional fry-up, served more often these days at the weekend, when everyone has more time. The bacon is back bacon, more meaty and less fatty than American bacon. The sausages are thick and meaty, and the eggs good-quality and as large as possible.

Australians eat a similar breakfast to the British, with the unexpected addition of kangaroo sausages! You will also find popovers, and Australians love toast thickly covered with a strong-tasting, salty spread made from yeast extract. In New Zealand, most restaurants will have at least one menu option served with grilled bananas, a delicious accompaniment to French toast, which is good made with slightly aged Arizmendi bread.

equipment

You do not need a lot of special equipment for making breakfast. At least one good-quality large skillet, preferably nonstick and oven-safe, is a must. You probably already have pots, sheet pans, and baking pans (9x13 inches is about the right size for many of these recipes, although a couple use a slightly smaller one).

For smoothies, you will need a blender (one that crushes ice would be helpful). Pancakes can be made in a large skillet, or on a griddle, and waffles have to be made in a waffle iron. For muffins you need a 12-cup muffin pan, and use paper muffin liners—these keep the muffins together nicely.

When making yeast bread, it is very easy to learn the technique of kneading; however, a freestanding tabletop mixer gets the job done quickly and efficiently. It will turn out perfect bread every time.

You will need a whisk for whisking eggs, although for lightly beaten eggs you can use a dinner fork. A pastry brush to apply oil, butter, and various toppings will be needed as well.

ingredients

The ingredients needed to make the recipes in this book are pretty standard fare for most kitchens. I do, however, call for buttermilk in my baked goods, which might be new to you.

buttermilk

Buttermilk is a wonderful dairy product that makes delicious baked goods. It was first called buttermilk because it was originally the liquid left over after the butter-churning process was finished. Despite its name, it is low in fat.

It is a rich-tasting, thick, and tangy milk, with a buttery flavor. Like yogurt and sour cream, it helps tenderize the gluten in a batter, giving a softer texture and more body, and helping baked goods to rise. It gives a pleasant tang and buttery flavor to pancakes and baked goods, without adding lots of butter or fat. Buttermilk is acidic, so baking soda is added to the recipe to balance the acid.

Buttermilk is sold in smaller containers than milk, and it has a longer shelf life, so you have more time to use it. It tends to thicken with time, so shake the carton before use.

eggs

Use the freshest eggs for poaching and frying and leave the less fresh for baking. Buy organic eggs if you can; they have higher levels of vitamins E and A, and they taste better and have a richer color.

There are three ways to test whether an egg is fresh. First, hold the egg in your hand and shake gently. If you feel a rattle, it is not very fresh. In a newly laid egg, the air cell within the egg is very small, the white cushions the yolk, and the egg feels solid and quite heavy when shaken.

The second way is to gently drop the egg, without breaking, into a deep bowl of water. If the egg immediately sinks to the bottom and lies on its side, the egg is fresh. As an egg ages, more air permeates the shell, and it will begin to float and stand upright. If it floats without touching the bottom of the bowl at all, do not eat it as it is probably bad.

The third way to test for freshness is to break the egg onto a flat plate. A fresh yolk will sit high on the white in the middle and the white will be thick and stay close to the yolk. As an egg gets older, the white becomes more runny and will spread over the plate, and the yolk will break more easily. If the white is cloudy, it means the egg is very fresh. Store eggs in the refrigerator for up to one month, in the carton, which helps prevent them absorbing food odors.

meats

All the meats used in this book can be found in ordinary supermarkets. Use the best-quality bacon and sausages you can find. I've included a recipe for making your own sausage, which allows you to control the amount of fat, salt, and preservatives that you eat.

oils, butter & margarine

You can use most oils, butter, or margarine for most of these recipes. My personal preference is canola oil. If you have heart problems, you need to keep your consumption of hard fats like butter and margarine to a minimum. Much better for you is a fat that is runny when cold, and canola oil is the best of the lot. It's even better than olive oil, which although better for you than butter, is quite strong-tasting. It has too powerful a flavor for cooking pancakes and waffles. You can also use sunflower oil, a delicate oil ideal for cooking pancakes or using in muffins. If you are trying to keep to a low-fat diet, it is quite acceptable to use a spray oil in your skillet.

flour & sugar

All recipes in this book use all-purpose flour, unless otherwise specified. Use the type of sugar called for in the recipes. When it is not specified, granulated sugar is intended.

nuts, seeds & dried fruits

Nuts and seeds add amazing variety and crunch to bread, cereals, muffins, and even pancakes and waffles. Walnuts especially are good for your heart, but not too many as they are high in calories (four walnuts a day is ideal). The nuts and seeds used in these recipes are unroasted and unsalted and should be easy to find. Keep them in an airtight container, in a cool place, for optimum freshness. Dried fruits also need to be kept in airtight containers in a cool place.

techniques

muffins

The secret to good muffins is a very simple one. Mix all the wet ingredients in one bowl, and all the dry ingredients in another bowl. Treat fresh fruit as a dry ingredient, canned fruit as wet (except for canned or very ripe blueberries, which have to be added at the last possible moment because they crush very easily).

When you have your ingredients ready in their bowls, make a well in the center of the dry ingredients with a metal spoon or a fork, and pour the wet ingredients into the middle. Fold the two together as quickly and lightly as you can, until they are just blended. Do not worry about small dry lumps that may remain. Spoon batter into paper-lined muffin pans immediately, filling the cups about 3/4 full. Put the pan directly into the oven. The end result will be light and airy muffins.

pancakes

The same idea works for pancakes too. Mix dry ingredients in one bowl, wet in another, and then mix together as with muffins. The small lumps do not matter; it is more important to work the batter as little as possible. After making one or two pancakes, you will begin to get an idea of what to watch for when cooking them.

When you have spooned a measure of batter into the skillet and it sizzles and begins to cook, it will start to form small bubbles and look dry around the edge of the pancake. It will start to rise very slightly in the middle, and that is the time to turn it over. It will start to look light and risen as it cooks. When the pancake is done, it should be a lovely golden brown color and feel considerably lighter as you lift it.

crêpes

Unlike pancakes, the thinner crêpe has a different look and feel. It is quicker to cook and easier to burn. It takes a little more practice to perfect the technique for a crêpe, but after making one or two, you will get the idea very quickly.

The batter needs to be spooned into the lightly oiled skillet, and then swirled around the pan so that it just covers the surface. The skillet should be very hot (not smoking) before you pour in the batter, then you need to get it back on the heat immediately. Be careful, because it will cook quickly, but it should not stick. It should be easy to flip over to cook the other side.

bread

All around the world, bread is the popular choice for breakfast. Once you have mastered the art of bread making, you will be hooked. As mentioned earlier, a freestanding tabletop mixer is a handy appliance to have in your kitchen, but kneading dough by hand is a satisfying occupation. You start making yeast bread with a yeast liquid. Add a teaspoon of sugar to warm water or milk, and add dry yeast. Let the liquid stand for about 15 minutes, until it is very frothy. The better the froth, the better the rise of the dough. (The dough should never rise more than double in size, however.)

When you are mixing your dough, watch the consistency of the flour and water. If the dough is too sticky (it sticks to your fingers), add a little more flour. If the dough seems too dry, add a tiny bit more water. Place the dough on a floured surface, and lightly flour your hands. Push the heel of your hands into the middle of the dough with a sharp movement, almost like a punch. Slightly roll the dough as you do so. With each push, turn the dough a half turn and knead again. Continue working the dough with your fingers and knuckles, until it becomes smooth and elastic. This is a technique that is quickly acquired once you start the process.

When the dough feels smooth, place it in a large, greased bowl, and turn the dough over so that it is completely covered with a thin film of oil. This is to stop it from forming a hard crust. Cover the bowl with plastic wrap and set it aside to rise until the dough has doubled in size. If you have time to let it rise, leave it at room temperature. If you have a lot of time, leave it overnight in the refrigerator; if you are short on time, leave it in a warm place.

When it has doubled in size, put the dough onto a lightly floured surface, punch down to remove air bubbles, and then follow the specific recipe.

drinks, smoothies & yogurt

Fruit juices and smoothies are a great way of getting children to eat fruit and vegetables. For the grownups, sophisticated coffee and smooth, rich, decadent hot chocolate are delicious alternatives. Try a bellini or Bloody Mary for celebrations and weekend treats.

wake-up juice

see variations page 45

Start the day off right by firing up the circulation and kicking off the body's cleansing process.

2 large oranges   1/2 cup fresh strawberries
1 pink grapefruit   1/2 banana

Squeeze the juice from the oranges and grapefruit. Pour juice into a blender, add the strawberries and banana, and blend well. Pour the juice into glasses, and serve.

Serves 2

bloody mary

see variations page 46

The Bloody Mary is great as a starter for any breakfast or brunch. It is also great as a hangover cure!

1/4 cup vodka
1/2 cup tomato juice
1 tbsp. lemon juice
2 dashes Worcestershire sauce

2 drops hot pepper sauce, such as Tabasco
pinch salt
pinch freshly ground black pepper
celery stalk, to garnish

Place all the ingredients, except the celery, into a cocktail shaker with 3 cubes of ice and shake well. Strain into a highball glass, being careful not to allow any ice to fall into the glass as this would dilute the cocktail. Garnish with the celery stick, which you eat between sips to enhance the flavor.

Serves 1

celebration breakfast bellini

see variations page 47

Traditionally this cocktail is made with puréed white peaches and Italian sparkling wine, with a little raspberry or cherry juice to give it a pink glow. Ideally you want one-third peach purée to two-thirds champagne.

2 ripe peaches, peeled, halved, and pitted
2 tsp. raspberry juice (optional)
chilled champagne

Chill 2 champagne glasses in your refrigerator. Put the peaches in a blender and purée until completely smooth. Spoon about 1/4 cup of the purée into a chilled champagne glass, add the raspberry juice if using, and top off with champagne. Serve immediately.

Serves 2

easy home-brewed cappuccino

see variations page 48

A French press, sometimes called a cafetière, works well for this recipe. You'll also need a handheld stick whisk.

coffee beans
1 cup milk
1 tsp. sugar, or to taste
1 tsp. grated semisweet (or a favorite)
    chocolate, for sprinkling

Make enough coffee for 2 mugs in a French press or your favorite coffeemaker, following the directions. Grind the beans just before you need them and use extra beans so your coffee is extra-strong.

Microwave the milk and sugar in a glass microwave-safe cup until almost boiling. Alternatively, heat it in a small saucepan on top of the stove. Pour 3/4 cup of the hot sweetened milk into your mug with the coffee. Use your handheld whisk to whip the remaining 1/4 cup milk in the glass cup until frothy, then pour it on top of the coffee. Sprinkle with grated chocolate.

Serves 2

spiced hot coffee

see variations page 49

Plain coffee is delicious, but sometimes you just want something different—especially on a cold winter day when you need some extra heat.

1 cup water
1 cinnamon stick
6 cardamom pods, split
6 black peppercorns
1/2 cup heavy cream

3 tbsp. brown sugar
2 cups freshly brewed coffee
freshly grated nutmeg, to serve

In a small saucepan, combine the water and the spices. Bring to a boil, then reduce the heat and simmer for 5 minutes. Add the cream and sugar and stir. Add the coffee, increase the heat, and bring to just under boiling. Remove from the heat and strain into mugs. Serve immediately, sprinkled with nutmeg.

Serves 1-2

rich & creamy hot chocolate

see variations page 50

The better the quality of chocolate used, the better the taste. Always use whole milk to get a fuller, more rounded, creamy flavor.

3 1/2 cups whole milk
1/4 cup half-and-half
1/4 cup unsweetened cocoa powder
1/2 cup sugar
pinch salt

4 oz. bittersweet or semisweet chocolate,
  chopped
whipped cream and miniature marshmallows,
  to serve

In a medium saucepan, bring the milk and half-and-half to just simmering with the cocoa, sugar, and salt. Add the chopped chocolate, whisking all the time until the mixture becomes frothy. Ladle into 4 mugs, and top with whipped cream and marshmallows.

Serves 4

mocha shake

see variations page 51

If you can never decide between coffee and chocolate, this will solve your problem. It's rich, thick, and absolutely divine.

3 1/2 cups milk
3 1/2 oz. semisweet chocolate, broken

1 tbsp. instant espresso granules
4 scoops vanilla ice cream

Bring 1 1/2 cups of milk almost to a boil in a saucepan, then add the chocolate and the espresso granules, and stir until melted. Set aside to cool.

Just before serving, pour the mixture into a blender with the ice cream and the rest of the milk, and blend until smooth.

Serves 3-4

multi-berry smoothie

see variations page 52

Mixed berry smoothies contain a high level of antioxidants and vitamins, so not only are they good for you, but they also taste wonderful. If you use frozen berries, you'll have a frozen smoothie, a great way to treat yourself on a hot summer day.

1/2 cup fresh or frozen blueberries
1/2 cup fresh or frozen strawberries
1/2 cup fresh or frozen raspberries
3/4 cup milk (whole or low-fat)
2 tbsp. low-fat plain yogurt

2 tbsp. freshly squeezed orange juice
1 tbsp. honey
1 tbsp. wheat germ
a little sugar to taste (optional)

Put the blueberries into a blender and purée until smooth. Add the strawberries and raspberries and blend again. Add the rest of the ingredients, blend, and then pour into glasses and serve.

Serves 2

protein smoothie

see variations page 53

The protein powder in this smoothie helps you start your day feeling energized.

1 banana
1/2 mango, peeled, seeded, and chopped
1/2 cup chopped fresh or canned pineapple
1 serving protein powder

1/2 cup orange juice (preferably freshly
   squeezed)
4 ice cubes

Put the fruits together in a blender and blend briefly. Add the protein powder (checking directions on the package) and blend again. Add the orange juice, blend, and then add the ice cubes and blend again until smooth. Pour into a large glass and serve.

Serves 1

greek yogurt

see variations page 54

This might, at first glance, look complicated, but the effort is well worth it. Remember to keep a small amount of yogurt aside to make the next batch.

4 cups plus 3 tbsp. whole milk, either sheep
    or cow's
3 tbsp. live-culture yogurt

Have all the ingredients at room temperature. Heat 4 cups milk just to the boiling point, then pour milk into a nonmetallic container. Let cool to lukewarm, about 110°F. A skin will form on top as the milk cools.

Mix the yogurt with the remaining 3 tablespoons room-temperature milk, then add the mixture to the lukewarm milk, carefully pouring it into the bowl down the sides so that you do not disturb the skin on top. Cover bowl with a clean dishtowel and place it on another dishtowel in a warm dry place for at least 8 hours, or overnight, until it thickens (8–12 hours is best). The longer you leave the yogurt after 12 hours, the more sour it will become.

Carefully drain off any excess liquid. Refrigerate for at least 4 hours before serving. It will keep for 4-5 days. Remember to save a small amount to make the next batch!

You can eat the yogurt, as well as the skin on top, now. Alternatively, you can proceed to the next step to make the thick yogurt used in so many Greek recipes. Line a large bowl with a piece of cheesecloth or a clean white dishtowel. Pour the yogurt into the center of the cloth. Bring the four corners of the cloth together and lift the yogurt. Over the sink, twist the

corners to squeeze out the liquid through the cloth. When you have forced out the majority of the liquid, tie off the top of the cloth, above the mass of yogurt, with string.

Place in a colander or sieve over a bowl so the liquid can continue to drain, and place the whole thing in the refrigerator for 2-3 hours. After draining, put the cloth with the yogurt inside the sink and with your hands, force out any remaining liquid. Remove the string, open the cloth, and, using a spatula, put the yogurt in a bowl for use. The yogurt should have the consistency of sour cream.

Makes about 2 cups

apricot–oat smoothie

see variations page 55

Smoothies made with oats satisfy hunger and help lower cholesterol. Strong-tasting spices also help to make you feel full.

1 1/2 cups canned apricots, drained
3 tbsp. quick-cooking oats
1 1/2 cups cold milk

1 tsp. ground ginger
1 tsp. ground cinnamon
1 tbsp. honey

Put the apricots into a blender and purée. Add all the other ingredients and blend until smooth. Pour into glasses and serve.

Serves 2

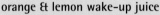
variations

wake-up juice

see base recipe page 27

orange & lemon wake-up juice
Prepare the basic recipe, omitting the grapefruit and adding the juice of 2 more oranges and 1 lemon.

orange, lemon & pineapple wake-up juice
Prepare the basic recipe, omitting the grapefruit and adding the juice of 1/2 lemon. Add 1 cup chopped canned or fresh pineapple and blend until smooth.

orange & cranberry wake-up juice
Prepare the basic recipe, omitting the grapefruit and substituting 2 cups fresh or frozen cranberries. Add a little sugar, if desired, to taste.

mixed berry wake-up juice
Prepare the basic recipe, omitting the grapefruit and adding 1 cup fresh or frozen mixed berries.

tropical wake-up juice
Prepare the basic recipe, omitting the grapefruit. Substitute 1/2 mango, peeled, pitted, and chopped; 1 cup chopped pineapple; and another 1/2 banana.

variations

bloody mary

see base recipe page 28

bloody maria
Prepare the basic recipe, replacing the vodka with 1/4 cup tequila.

bloody mary with cilantro
Prepare the basic recipe, adding 1 teaspoon finely chopped fresh cilantro.

mustard mary
Prepare the basic recipe, adding 1/2 teaspoon French mustard (a strong, dark mustard).

virgin mary
Prepare the basic recipe, omitting the vodka.

soy sauce mary
Prepare the basic recipe, replacing the Worcestershire sauce with dark soy sauce.

variations

celebration breakfast bellini

see base recipe page 31

italian bellini
Prepare the basic recipe, replacing the champagne with Italian sparkling wine.

bellini martini
Instead of the basic recipe, pour 1/4 cup vodka and 1/4 cup peach schnapps into a cocktail shaker with 1 cup ice. Shake until frothy, then strain into a martini glass. Top the glass off with about 1/4 cup champagne. Garnish with 3 fresh raspberries.

virgin bellini
Prepare the basic recipe, replacing the champagne with sparkling apple cider.

frozen bellini
Instead of the basic recipe, blend 1 part peach schnapps with 3 parts champagne, and freeze until slushy, about 2 hours. In a large glass, put a canned or peeled fresh peach half, add 1/2 cup slush, and carefully pour a little sangria on top to add a dash of color.

variations

easy home-brewed cappuccino

see base recipe page 32

vanilla cappuccino
Prepare the basic recipe, adding 1 teaspoon vanilla extract to each mug along with the milk and coffee.

iced cappuccino
Prepare the basic recipe, replacing 1/4 cup of the milk with 1/4 cup heavy cream and making the coffee double strength. Allow the cappuccino to cool to room temperature, then put all the ingredients in a blender with 4 ice cubes and blend until smooth.

cinnamon-spiced cappuccino
Prepare the basic recipe, adding 1 teaspoon ground cinnamon to the mug with the milk and coffee. Replace the chocolate with a sprinkling of ground cinnamon.

chocolate-orange cappuccino
Prepare the basic recipe, replacing the grated chocolate with plenty of grated orange-flavored chocolate.

ginger-spiced cappuccino
Prepare the basic recipe, adding 1 teaspoon ground ginger to the mug with the milk and coffee.

variations

spiced hot coffee

see base recipe page 34

nutmeg-spiced coffee
Prepare the basic recipe, replacing the cardamom pods and black peppercorns with 1/4 teaspoon ground cloves and 1/4 teaspoon ground nutmeg.

vanilla-spiced coffee
Prepare the basic recipe, omitting the cardamom pods and black peppercorns and adding 1/2 teaspoon vanilla extract.

fall-spiced coffee
Prepare the basic recipe, replacing the cardamom pods and black peppercorns with 1/4 teaspoon pumpkin pie spice.

honey-spiced coffee
Prepare the basic recipe, omitting the cardamom pods and black peppercorns and adding 2 teaspoons honey.

cocoa-spiced coffee
Prepare the basic recipe, omitting the cardamom pods and black peppercorns and adding 1/2 teaspoon vanilla extract and 1 teaspoon unsweetened cocoa powder.

variations

rich & creamy hot chocolate

see base recipe page 35

rich & creamy hot chocolate with cinnamon
Prepare the basic recipe, and add a cinnamon stick to each mug as
you serve.

rich & creamy hot chocolate with vanilla
Prepare the basic recipe, and add 1 teaspoon vanilla extract to the saucepan
just before serving.

rich & creamy hot chocolate with grand marnier
Prepare the basic recipe, and add 2 tablespoons Grand Marnier to the
saucepan just before serving.

rich, creamy & spicy hot chocolate
Prepare the basic recipe, and add 1/2 teaspoon chili powder to the saucepan
just before serving.

fudgy, rich & creamy hot chocolate
Prepare the basic recipe, replacing half the sugar with brown sugar. (It may
not sound very different, but the brown sugar makes the hot chocolate taste
like chocolate fudge.)

variations

mocha shake

see base recipe page 37

double chocolate shake
Prepare the basic recipe, replacing the espresso granules and the vanilla ice cream with 4 scoops of chocolate ice cream.

chocolate cherry shake
Prepare the basic recipe, replacing the espresso granules and the vanilla ice cream with 4 scoops of cherry ice cream and 1/4 cup fresh or canned pitted cherries.

nondairy chocolate coconut shake
Prepare the basic recipe, replacing the milk with 3 cups coconut milk. Check that the semisweet chocolate you use contains no dairy products.

mocha banana shake
Prepare the basic recipe, adding 1 banana to the ingredients.

rich mocha shake
Prepare the basic recipe, using only 2 1/2 cups milk and adding 1/2 cup heavy cream.

variations

multi-berry smoothie

see base recipe page 38

apple blackberry smoothie
Prepare the basic recipe, omitting the blueberries. Add 1/2 peeled and
chopped apple and 1/2 cup blackberries. Add a little extra sugar to taste,
if desired.

nondairy berry smoothie
Prepare the basic recipe, replacing the milk and the yogurt with coconut
milk and soy yogurt.

quick berry banana smoothie
Prepare the basic recipe, omitting the milk, honey, and wheat germ.
Increase the amount of yogurt and orange juice to 1 cup of each, and
add 1/2 banana.

tropical smoothie
Prepare the basic recipe, omitting the orange juice and blueberries and
adding 1/2 cup chopped fresh or canned pineapple and 1/2 mango, peeled,
pitted, and chopped.

protein smoothie

see base recipe page 41

dairy peach melba protein smoothie
Prepare the basic recipe, omitting the orange juice, pineapple, and mango.
Substitute 1 cup sliced and peeled fresh or canned peaches, 1/4 cup fresh
raspberries, and 1/2 cup whole milk.

piña colada protein smoothie
Prepare the basic recipe, omitting the orange juice and mango and adding
1/2 cup coconut milk, 2 tablespoons coconut cream, and another 1/4 cup
chopped pineapple.

tropical protein smoothie
Prepare the basic recipe, omitting the orange juice and adding 1 cup Greek
yogurt (page 42) and 1 cup canned tropical fruit salad, drained.

strawberry protein smoothie
Prepare the basic recipe, omitting the pineapple and mango and adding
1 cup fresh strawberries and 1 tablespoon strawberry jam.

greek yogurt

see base recipe page 42

honey yogurt
Prepare the basic recipe. To serve, swirl 1 tablespoon of honey through each serving.

peach melba
Prepare the basic recipe. Put 3 or 4 slices of canned or fresh peaches into individual dishes, then spoon about 1/2 cup yogurt over the peaches. Finish each serving with a few fresh raspberries.

cereal-enriched yogurt
Prepare the basic recipe. Swirl 3 tablespoons Cherry-Berry Granola Crunch (page 65) per person through the yogurt, just before serving.

strawberry yogurt
Prepare the basic recipe. For each serving, crush 1/2 cup fresh or frozen strawberries, mix with 1 tablespoon strawberry jam, and stir into the yogurt. Add a special twist, if you wish, by serving the yogurt in parfait glasses, layered alternating with a few extra fresh strawberries and some granola.

apricot–oat smoothie

see base recipe page 44

peach–oat smoothie
Prepare the basic recipe, replacing the apricots with 1 cup fresh or canned peach slices. Omit the cinnamon.

nondairy apricot–oat smoothie
Prepare the basic recipe, replacing the milk with oat milk.

pineapple–oat smoothie
Prepare the basic recipe, omitting the apricots, ginger, and cinnamon. Substitute 1 cup sliced canned or fresh pineapple and 2 tablespoons coconut cream.

raspberry–oat smoothie
Prepare the basic recipe, omitting the apricots and ginger. Substitute 1 cup fresh raspberries and 1 tablespoon raspberry jam.

swiss muesli smoothie
Prepare the basic recipe, omitting the apricots and ginger. Add 1 cup dried apples, 2 tablespoons wheat germ, and 1 teaspoon vanilla extract.

cereals &
breakfast bars

Whether they're in a bar or a bowl, wholegrain

cereals are very good for our bodies. The fiber is

necessary to keep your equilibrium in trim, and you

will certainly notice a difference if you start

incorporating whole grains into your daily breakfast.

two-in-one muesli

see variations page 74

Muesli cold or muesli hot with oats—this recipe gives you two ways to enjoy muesli. You start by making a basic muesli mix (which is delicious by itself, perhaps topped with a spoonful of yogurt). When you want a hot cereal, you cook some of the mix with milk and extra oats.

for the muesli mix
2 1/2 cups rolled oats
1 cup whole wheat flakes (preferably toasted whole wheat flakes and flaxseed cereal)
1 cup low-fat granola with raisins
1/2 cup dried berries
1/4 cup golden raisins
3 tablespoons sesame seeds
1/4 cup chopped walnuts

for the hot muesli oatmeal
2 cups whole milk
1 cup muesli mix
1/4 cup rolled oats
2 tablespoons sugar, or to taste
1 sliced banana, to serve

First make the muesli mix. In a large bowl, mix all the muesli ingredients, stirring until they are combined well. This makes about 5 1/2 cups muesli mix. Store in an airtight container.

To make the hot muesli oatmeal, in a medium saucepan, heat the milk and the muesli mix with the extra rolled oats. Cook over medium heat, stirring constantly, until the milk has been incorporated into the cereal. Add sugar, to taste. Serve immediately, with a sliced banana on top.

Serves 2 (hot cereal)

honey muesli with raspberries & hazelnuts

see variations page 75

After making your own cereal, store-bought will never taste good enough again.

2 cups rolled oats
1/2 cup wheat germ
1/2 cup freshly squeezed orange juice
1/2 cup raisins

1/2 cup hazelnuts, toasted
3 tbsp. honey
fresh raspberries, to serve

In a large bowl, mix together the oats and wheat germ, stir in the orange juice, and cover. Let soak overnight.

In the morning, add the raisins and hazelnuts. Drizzle with the honey. Spoon into bowls and sprinkle a few raspberries on top.

The muesli can be stored, without the raspberries, in an airtight container.

Serves 4-5

healthy cereal

see variations page 76

With all its nuts and seeds, this cereal has a wonderful texture and crunch.

2 1/2 cups rolled oats
1/4 cup sesame seeds
1 cup chopped mixed nuts
2/3 cup wheat germ
2/3 cup unsweetened shredded coconut
1/2 cup sunflower seeds

1/2 cup brown sugar
2/3 cup sunflower or any light oil
2/3 cup water
1/4 tsp. salt
1 tsp. vanilla extract

Preheat the oven to 350°F.

Combine the oats, sesame seeds, nuts, wheat germ, coconut, sunflower seeds, and brown sugar in a large bowl. In a medium bowl, whisk together the oil, water, salt, and vanilla extract. Stir the liquid mixture into the dry ingredients, mixing well. Spread mixture into a large roasting pan or over a cookie sheet and bake for 20-30 minutes, stirring occasionally, until crisp and golden.

Remove from oven and let cool, before storing in an airtight container.

Serves 6-8

great-for-you granola

see variations page 77

Do not be tempted to use ordinary barley in this recipe; it will be far too hard and crunchy. Just leave it out if the quick-cooking variety is not available.

7 cups rolled oats
1/2 cup wheat germ
1/2 cup wheat bran
1 cup sunflower seeds
1 1/2 cups chopped mixed nuts
1/2 cup quick-cooking barley (optional)
3/4 cup brown sugar
3/4 cup water
1/2 cup sunflower or canola oil

1/4 cup honey
1/4 cup molasses
pinch salt
1 tsp. ground cinnamon
1 tsp. ground nutmeg
1 tbsp. vanilla extract
1 1/2 cups mixed dried tropical fruit, such as
    pineapple, mango, figs, and dates

Preheat the oven to 300°F. In a large bowl, mix together the oats, wheat germ, wheat bran, sunflower seeds, nuts, and barley.

In a large saucepan, combine the brown sugar, water, oil, honey, molasses, salt, cinnamon, nutmeg, and vanilla. Heat gently until the sugar is dissolved; do not boil. Cool slightly. Pour the syrup over the dry ingredients and stir well until thoroughly mixed. Spread mixture onto two cookie sheets in a thin layer and bake for about 45 minutes, stirring occasionally.

Remove from the oven and immediately add the dried fruit, stirring it in well. Let granola cool on the cookie sheets, then store in an airtight container.

Makes about 11 cups

fruity sesame seed cereal

see variations page 78

There are countless combinations of oats, nuts, and fruits to make your breakfast cereals enticing.

1/3 cup sunflower oil or another light oil
1/3 cup apple cider
4 tbsp. honey
1 tsp. ground cinnamon
2 1/2 cups rolled oats

1 cup chopped raw cashews
1/2 cup sliced almonds
1/2 cup sesame seeds
3/4 cup raisins
3/4 cup dried cranberries

Preheat the oven to 350°F. Put the oil, apple cider, honey, and cinnamon in a large saucepan. Bring to a boil, stirring constantly. Stir in the oats, nuts, and seeds, and combine well. Spread the mixture evenly over a cookie sheet or into a large roasting pan. Bake for about 20 minutes, stirring occasionally. Remove pan from the oven and stir in the raisins and cranberries. Let cool, then store in an airtight container.

Makes about 6 cups

cherry–berry granola crunch

see variations page 79

The aroma of this granola baking in the oven is so appetizing you won't want to wait until morning!

2 tbsp. sunflower or another light oil
1/2 cup maple syrup
2 tbsp. honey
1 tsp. vanilla extract
3 1/2 cups rolled oats

1/2 cup sunflower seeds
1/2 cup pumpkin seeds
4 tbsp. sesame seeds
1 cup mixed dried cherries and berries
2/3 cup unsweetened shredded coconut

Preheat the oven to 300°F. Mix the oil, maple syrup, honey, and vanilla in a large bowl. Add the oats and sunflower, pumpkin, and sesame seeds, and mix well. Spread the granola in a large roasting pan and bake for 15 minutes. Remove pan from oven, mix in the dried fruit and coconut, and put back in the oven for 10 more minutes. Remove from the oven and let granola cool in the pan. Store in an airtight container.

Makes about 5 cups

power bars

see variations page 80

Having coffee in these bars gives a caffeine boost in the morning. They're great for people with no time to spare. Just wrap and go.

1 cup chopped pecans
1 cup slivered almonds
2/3 cup unsweetened shredded coconut
1 1/2 cups rolled oats
1 1/2 cups unsweetened rice cereal, such as
   Rice Krispies

1 cup light corn syrup
1/4 cup brown sugar
pinch salt
2 tbsp. freshly ground coffee
1 tsp. vanilla extract

Preheat the oven to 350°F. Toast the nuts and coconut for 6-7 minutes on a cookie sheet, until the coconut is golden, stirring it once or twice. Watch carefully so that it does not burn. In a large bowl, combine the toasted nuts and coconut with the oats and rice cereal. Set aside.

Grease an 8-inch square baking pan with a little vegetable oil. In a saucepan, heat together the syrup, brown sugar, salt, coffee, and vanilla. Bring to a boil, stirring constantly. The mixture will thicken slightly as it cooks. Remove the pan from the heat and pour the syrup over the cereal mixture. Stir well to combine. Spread the mixture evenly in the greased baking pan, then let it cool to room temperature before cutting into bars.

Makes 9 bars

cranberry happy bars

see variations page 81

There is enough goodness in these bars to keep you on the go until lunch.

1 (14-oz.) can condensed milk
1 1/2 cups rolled oats
2/3 cup unsweetened shredded coconut
1/2 cup dried cranberries

1/3 cup pumpkin seeds
1/3 cup sunflower seeds
1/3 cup sesame seeds
2/3 cup chopped mixed nuts

Preheat the oven to 270°F and grease a 9x13-inch baking pan. In a large saucepan, gently warm the condensed milk. In a large bowl, combine all the other ingredients, then stir them into the warm condensed milk. Spread the mixture in the baking pan, pressing down to smooth the surface.

Bake for 1 hour, then remove pan from the oven. Cool in the pan for 15 minutes, then cut into 16 bars and let cool completely before serving.

Makes 16 bars

english flapjacks

see variations page 82

Known in England as "flapjacks," these are delicious and crunchy bar cookies made with oats. They couldn't be easier to make.

1/2 cup butter, plus extra for greasing
1/2 cup sugar
4 tbsp. golden syrup or dark corn syrup
1 1/2 cups rolled oats

1 tsp. baking powder
1/2 tsp. salt
1 large egg, lightly beaten

Preheat the oven to 375°F. Grease a shallow 8x8-inch baking pan and line it with parchment paper. Put the butter, sugar, and syrup into a medium saucepan and heat gently until the butter has melted. Stir in the remaining ingredients, and press the mixture into the baking pan. Bake for 20 minutes or until just golden at the edges. Remove from the oven and cool for 10 minutes.

Cut into bars in the pan and let sit until cold before removing.

Makes 16 bars

apple & almond bars

see variations page 83

Apples and almonds are a heavenly combination in this cakelike breakfast bar.

for the base and topping
2 cups all-purpose flour
1/2 tsp. baking powder
1 cup butter
1/2 cup sugar
1/2 tsp. salt
1/2 cup sliced almonds
2 egg yolks, lightly beaten
1 tsp. almond extract

for the filling
3/4 cup sugar
1/4 cup all-purpose flour
1 tsp. ground cinnamon
1/2 tsp. ground nutmeg
4 medium cooking apples,
    peeled, cored, and sliced

for the icing
1 tbsp. milk
1/2 tsp. almond extract
3/4 cup sifted powdered sugar

Preheat the oven to 350°F. Sift the flour and baking powder into a large bowl. Cut in the butter, using a pastry blender or your hands, until the pieces are the size of small peas. Add the 1/2 cup sugar, salt, and almonds. Using a fork, stir in the egg yolks and the almond extract. Press half of the crumb mixture (about 2 cups) into the bottom of an ungreased 9x13-inch baking pan. Set aside.

For the filling stir together the sugar, flour, cinnamon, and nutmeg in a bowl. Add the sliced apples and toss to combine. Arrange the apples evenly over the crumb mixture in the pan and sprinkle the remaining crumb mixture evenly over the top. Bake for 40 minutes, until the top is golden. Cool in the pan on a wire rack. In a small bowl, add the milk and almond extract to the powdered sugar and stir. Drizzle the icing over the top and let it set. Cut into bars.

Makes 24

variations

two-in-one muesli

see base recipe page 57

cold muesli mix & berries
Prepare the basic muesli mix and serve it cold, mixed with cold milk, and topped with fresh berries.

cold muesli mix with macadamia nuts & coconut
Prepare the basic muesli mix, replacing the walnuts with chopped macadamia nuts and adding 1/2 cup unsweetened flaked coconut.

hot muesli oatmeal with pecans & pineapple
Prepare the basic muesli mix, replacing the walnuts with pecans and adding 1/4 cup dried chopped pineapple.

hot muesli oatmeal with spices & maple syrup
Prepare the basic muesli mix, adding 1/2 teaspoon pumpkin pie spice with the rolled oats. Serve with the sliced banana and a generous swirl of maple syrup.

variations

honey muesli with raspberries & hazelnuts

see base recipe page 58

honey muesli with figs & almonds
Prepare the basic recipe, replacing the hazelnuts with slivered almonds and the raisins with 1/2 cup dried figs.

honey muesli with coconut & chocolate
Prepare the basic recipe, omitting the raspberries. Add 1/2 cup unsweetened shredded coconut to the cereal mix and stir in 1/2 cup semisweet chocolate chips just before serving.

honey muesli with apricot & ginger
Prepare the basic recipe, omitting the raspberries. Add 2 teaspoons ground ginger to the cereal mixture. Just before serving, sprinkle cereal with 1/2 cup chopped fresh, canned, or dried apricots.

honey muesli with pears & cranberries
Prepare the basic recipe, replacing the raisins with 1/2 cup dried cranberries and the raspberries with 1/2 cup peeled, cored, and sliced pears.

honey muesli with pineapple & macadamia nuts
Prepare the basic recipe, replacing the raisins with 1/2 cup chopped macadamia nuts and the raspberries with 1/2 cup dried pineapple pieces.

variations

healthy cereal

see base recipe page 61

berry healthy cereal
Prepare the basic recipe, adding 1/2 cup dried berries (preferably a medley of berries) to the cereal when it is fresh from the oven. Stir in well.

apple healthy cereal
Prepare the basic recipe, omitting the coconut. Add 2 teaspoons ground cinnamon to the cereal mix with the nuts. Add 2/3 cup dried apple slices to the cereal when it is fresh from the oven. Stir them in well.

very seedy healthy cereal
Prepare the basic recipe, adding 1/4 cup flaxseeds and 1/4 cup pumpkin seeds to the cereal mix with the other seeds.

malted cereal
Prepare the basic recipe, adding 1/4 cup malted drink powder to the cereal mix with the oats.

variations

great-for-you granola

see base recipe page 62

great-for-you granola with flaxseed
Prepare the basic recipe, adding 1/4 cup ground flaxseed.

christmas granola
Prepare the basic recipe, omitting the barley. Replace the tropical fruit with 1/2 cup each of glacé cherries, dark raisins, and currants. Add 1 tablespoon dried mixed peel, if desired. Add an extra 1 teaspoon each of cinnamon and nutmeg.

autumnal granola
Prepare the basic recipe, replacing the tropical dried fruit with 1/2 cup each of dried apples, dried chopped apricots, and dried cranberries.

gingerbread granola
Prepare the basic recipe, adding 3 teaspoons ground ginger with the other spices.

great-for-you granola bars
Prepare the basic recipe. In a large saucepan, heat 3/4 cup butter and mix in the granola and 2 beaten eggs. Mix well and put into a greased 9x13 metal baking pan. Bake at 350°F for about 30 minutes, until golden.

variations

fruity sesame seed cereal

see base recipe page 64

walnut & banana sesame seed cereal
Prepare the basic recipe, replacing the cashews and raisins with
1 cup chopped walnuts and 1/2 cup dried banana chips.

currant & raisin sesame seed cereal
Prepare the basic recipe, replacing the raisins and cranberries with
3/4 cup currants and 3/4 cup golden raisins.

hazelnut & pecan sesame seed cereal
Prepare the basic recipe, replacing the cashews and sliced almonds with
1/2 cup hazelnuts and 1 cup chopped pecans.

tropical sesame seed cereal
Prepare the basic recipe, replacing the raisins and cranberries with
1/2 cup dried chopped apricots and 1/2 cup dried chopped dates.

crunchy banana, walnut & sesame seed cereal
Prepare the basic recipe, omitting the cashews. Add 1/4 cup dried banana
chips and 1 cup chopped walnuts.

cherry–berry granola crunch

see base recipe page 65

heart-happy crunchy granola
Prepare the basic recipe, replacing the sunflower oil with 2 tablespoons canola oil and adding 1/2 cup chopped walnuts and 1/4 cup dried banana chips.

pecan & hazelnut crunchy granola
Prepare the basic recipe, adding 1/2 cup chopped pecans and 1/2 cup chopped hazelnuts.

chocolate macadamia nut crunchy granola
Prepare the basic recipe, omitting the cherries and berries. Add 1/2 cup chopped macadamia nuts to the granola before cooking. When the granola has cooled, stir in 1 cup semisweet chocolate chips.

date & walnut crunchy granola
Prepare the basic recipe, omitting the cherries and berries. Add 1/2 cup chopped walnuts to the granola before cooking, and 1/2 cup chopped dried dates in the last 10 minutes of cooking.

variations

power bars

see base recipe page 66

maple power bars
Prepare the basic recipe, replacing the corn syrup with 1 cup maple syrup.

high-fiber power bars
Prepare the basic recipe, adding 1/4 cup wheat bran to the cereal mix with the toasted nuts and coconut.

chocolate chip power bars
Prepare the basic recipe, adding 1/4 cup semisweet chocolate chips to the cereal mix with the toasted nuts and coconut.

tropical power bars
Prepare the basic recipe, adding 1/4 cup dried tropical fruits to the cereal mix with the toasted nuts and coconut.

variations

cranberry happy bars

see base recipe page 68

raisin happy bars
Prepare the basic recipe, replacing the cranberries with 1/2 cup raisins.

pineapple & macadamia happy bars
Prepare the basic recipe, replacing the cranberries with 1/2 cup chopped
candied pineapple and the chopped mixed nuts with chopped macadamia nuts.

date & pecan happy bars
Prepare the basic recipe, replacing the cranberries with chopped dates and
the mixed nuts with 2/3 cup chopped pecans.

berry happy bars
Prepare the basic recipe, replacing the cranberries with 1/2 cup mixed dried
berries and cherries.

variations

english flapjacks

see base recipe page 71

coconut flapjacks
Prepare the basic recipe, adding 2/3 cup unsweetened shredded coconut.

almond flapjacks
Prepare the basic recipe, adding 1/4 cup ground almonds and 1/4 cup slivered almonds.

cherry flapjacks
Prepare the basic recipe, adding 1/4 cup glacé cherries and 1 teaspoon vanilla extract.

ginger flapjacks
Prepare the basic recipe, adding 1/4 cup crystallized ginger and 1 teaspoon ground ginger.

apricot & raisin flapjacks
Prepare the basic recipe, adding 1/4 cup chopped dried apricots and 1/4 cup raisins.

variations

apple & almond bars

see base recipe page 72

apricot & almond bars

Prepare the basic recipe, replacing the apples with 2 cups sliced apricots.
Instead of the basic icing, use an orange icing, made by blending together in
a small bowl 1/2 cup powdered sugar, 1/8 teaspoon ground cinnamon, and
3 or 4 teaspoons orange juice (enough to make a drizzling consistency).

cherry & almond bars

Prepare the basic recipe, replacing the apples with 2 cups fresh or canned
pitted cherries.

raspberry, apple & almond bars

Prepare the basic recipe, adding 1/2 cup fresh raspberries to the apples in
the filling. Instead of the basic icing, mix 1 cup sifted powdered sugar,
1 tablespoon melted butter, 1 teaspoon vanilla extract, 1/2 teaspoon ground
cinnamon, and 2–3 teaspoons milk (enough to make a drizzling consistency).

blackberry, apple & almond bars

Prepare the basic recipe, adding 1/2 cup fresh blackberries to the apples in
the filling.

breads

If you have never made bread before, now is the time to start. Not only does it smell divine as it bakes, the taste is heavenly. Besides, you can control what goes into it, and make it as healthy or indulgent as you want.

rustic loaf

see variations page 106

This is a quick mix basic bread loaf, an easy introduction to home bread making.

4 cups white bread flour
2 tsp. salt
4 tbsp. olive oil

1 envelope dry yeast
1 1/4 cups warm water (110°F)

Mix all the ingredients together in a large bowl, taking care not to add the yeast on top of the salt. Bring the dough together with your hands. If it feels a little sticky, add more flour, and if it fails to come together properly, add a little more water. Knead well with your hands and knuckles until the dough is soft, smooth, and elastic. Alternatively, knead the dough for 5 minutes in a freestanding tabletop mixer.

Put the dough into a greased bowl, then turn the dough so that the top is greased as well. This will stop a crust from forming while the dough rises. Cover bowl with plastic wrap and leave in a warm place until the dough has doubled in size.

Turn onto a lightly floured surface and knock back slightly. Mold into a round, slightly oval shape and place on a cookie sheet lined with parchment paper. Put a few diagonal slashes across the top and dust with white flour. Let rise again for another hour.

Heat the oven to 425°F. Bake the loaf for 30 minutes until golden brown. Remove from the oven. Tap the bottom of the loaf; if it sounds hollow, it is cooked. If not, return to the oven for another few minutes. Cool on a wire rack.

Makes 1 loaf

no-yeast soda bread

see variations page 107

This bread is excellent with cheese. It is quickly made and should be eaten very fresh, as it does not keep well.

3 cups all-purpose flour
2 level tsp. baking soda
2 level tsp. cream of tartar
1 level tsp. salt

2 tbsp. vegetable shortening
1-2 tsp. sugar (optional)
1 generous cup (9 fl. oz.) buttermilk
2 tbsp. whole milk

Preheat the oven to 400°F. Sift the flour, baking soda, cream of tartar, and salt into a large bowl. Cut the vegetable shortening up and rub it into the dry ingredients with your fingertips until the mixture resembles fine breadcrumbs. Mix in the sugar, if using. Make a well in the center of the flour, add the buttermilk and milk, and mix to a soft but manageable dough, working it with a round-bladed knife.

Turn the dough onto a lightly floured surface, knead it lightly, and shape it into a 7-inch round. Flatten it slightly with your hand. With the back of a knife, make a large cross across the loaf, set it on a floured cookie sheet, and bake in the center of the oven for about 30 minutes. Cool on a wire rack and serve.

Makes 1 loaf

multigrain bread

see variations page 108

Baking your own whole-grain bread can give you a better, healthier, and tastier loaf, and is so easy to do, especially if you have a freestanding tabletop mixer.

1 tsp. sugar
2/3 cup warm water (110°F)
1 envelope dry yeast
1 1/2 cups white bread flour
1 3/4 cups whole wheat flour
1/4 cup wheat germ
1/4 cup oat bran

1 1/2 tsp. salt
1/3 cup milk
3 tbsp. honey
3 tbsp. olive oil
1 tsp. salt mixed with 2 tbsp. water
cracked wheat or rolled oats, for sprinkling tops

Dissolve the sugar in the warm water and sprinkle the yeast on top. Set aside until frothy, about 10-15 minutes. In a large bowl, mix the flours, wheat germ, oat bran, and salt. Make a well in the center and pour in the yeast liquid and the milk, honey, and olive oil. Knead with your hands and knuckles to make a smooth, soft dough. Alternatively, knead in a freestanding tabletop mixer for 5 minutes. Shape the dough into a ball, and place on a greased cookie sheet. Brush top with salt and water mixture, and sprinkle with cracked wheat or oats. Cover with plastic wrap, and leave in a warm place until the dough has doubled in size, about 1 1/2 hours.

Meanwhile, preheat the oven to 400°F. Bake the bread for about 30 minutes, until nicely browned. Turn out and cool on a wire rack.

Makes 1 loaf

raisin bread

see variations page 109

This bread is delicious sliced and spread with butter. Kids love it!

2 1/2 cups all-purpose flour
1 envelope dry yeast
1 tsp. sugar
1/2 cup warm milk (110°F)
3 tbsp. cold unsalted butter
1/2 cup brown sugar

3/4 tsp. salt
1 tsp. ground cinnamon
1 tsp. ground nutmeg
3/4 cup raisins
1 large egg, lightly beaten

Measure 1/2 cup of the flour into a bowl. Add the yeast, sugar, and warm milk, mixing well. Set aside until frothy, about 20 minutes. Using a pastry blender or your fingertips, cut the butter into the remaining flour. Mix in the brown sugar, salt, spices, and raisins. Add the egg and the yeast liquid and combine well. Knead with your hands and knuckles on a lightly floured surface until you have a soft, smooth, and elastic dough. Alternatively knead the dough in a freestanding tabletop mixer for 5 minutes. Place the dough in a greased bowl, turning so that the dough is evenly coated, cover with plastic wrap, and leave at room temperature until doubled in size.

Turn dough out onto a lightly floured surface and knock back. Knead again and shape to fit a greased (1-lb.) loaf pan. Place pan in a greased plastic bag, tie bag loosely, and set aside to let rise to about 1 inch above the top of the loaf pan. Meanwhile, preheat the oven to 350°F. Brush with beaten egg and bake the loaf for 30 minutes or until golden brown. Let cool in the pan for 5 minutes, then turn out, and cool on a wire rack.

Makes 1 loaf

brötchen

see variations page 110

You could serve these traditional German white rolls as part of a continental breakfast, with lots of butter and strawberry jam. They also make great dinner rolls.

1 tsp. sugar
1 3/4 cups warm water (110°F)
1 envelope dry yeast

5 cups white bread flour
1 tsp. salt
2 tsp. vegetable shortening

Prepare the yeast liquid by dissolving the sugar in the water and sprinkling the yeast on top. Leave until frothy, about 10-15 minutes. Sift the flour and salt into a large bowl, then, using a pastry blender or your fingertips, cut in the vegetable shortening until it resembles fine breadcrumbs. Add the yeast liquid and work to a firm dough. Turn onto a lightly floured surface and knead thoroughly with your hands and knuckles, until you have a soft, smooth, and elastic dough. Alternatively knead the dough in a freestanding tabletop mixer for 5 minutes. Put the dough into a greased bowl, turning to coat it all over, and cover with plastic wrap. Let rise in a warm place until doubled in size.

Turn the dough onto a lightly floured surface and knock back slightly. Divide dough evenly into 18 pieces and shape them into balls. Press down hard at first with the palm of your hand, then ease up. Place the brötchen about 1 inch apart on cookie sheets. Cover with lightly oiled plastic wrap and leave for about 30 minutes at room temperature. Meanwhile, preheat the oven to 450°F. Remove the plastic wrap and bake the brötchen for 15–20 minutes. Remove from the oven and cool on a wire rack. Although these are terrific served the same day, they can be kept a few days and rewarmed before serving.

Makes 18

italian herb bread

see variations page 111

This bread, flavored with garlic and herbs, is especially delicious when sliced and buttered to accompany an omelet.

3/4 cup warm water (110°F)
1/2 cup warm milk (110°F)
1 1/2 tsp. sugar
1 envelope dry yeast
3 tbsp. olive oil
1 clove garlic, crushed

2 tsp. dried basil
1 tsp. dried oregano
1 tsp. dried thyme
5 cups white bread flour,
    plus extra to sprinkle
1 tsp. salt

Mix the warm water and warm milk in a small bowl, then add the sugar to dissolve. Sprinkle the yeast on top. Set aside until frothy, about 10-15 minutes. In a small skillet set over a low heat, warm the oil and sauté the garlic and herbs together gently. Do not heat the garlic too much or it will be bitter. Cool.

In a large bowl, mix the flour and the salt. Make a well in the center and add the yeast liquid and the garlic and herb mixture. Work to a soft dough. Turn out onto a lightly floured surface and knead, using your hands and knuckles, until you have a soft, smooth, and elastic dough. Alternatively, knead in a freestanding tabletop mixer for 5 minutes. Place the dough in a greased bowl and turn so that the dough is greased all over. Cover and let rise in a warm place until doubled. Turn the dough out onto a lightly floured surface, knock back, and knead a little more. Form dough into an oval about 8–10 inches long and place it on a floured cookie sheet. Cover and let rise again until doubled. Heat the oven to 400°F. Remove cover and bake the bread for about 30 minutes. Cool on a wire rack. Sprinkle with flour to serve.

Makes 1 loaf

pumpkin swirl bread

see variations page 112

This wonderful breakfast bread is even more delicious when made into French toast.

butter, for greasing
1 tsp. sugar
1/4 cup warm water (110°F)
1 envelope dry yeast
3 1/2 cups white bread flour
1 tsp. ground cinnamon
1 tsp. ground ginger
1/4 tsp. ground cloves
1 tsp. ground allspice
1 tsp. salt

3 tbsp. sunflower oil, plus extra for greasing
1/3 cup warm milk
1 cup pumpkin purée
1/4 cup brown sugar
1/2 cup raisins
1/2 cup chopped walnuts
2 tbsp. melted butter
2 tbsp. sugar mixed with 2 tsp. ground
    cinnamon
1 egg, beaten with a little milk

Grease a 2-lb. bread pan with butter. Prepare the yeast liquid by dissolving sugar in warm water and sprinkling yeast on top. Leave until frothy, about 10-15 minutes. In a large bowl, combine 3 cups of the flour with the spices and salt. In a separate bowl, mix 3 tablespoons oil, warm milk, pumpkin purée, and brown sugar. Add to the flour with yeast liquid, then work the ingredients into a soft dough. Turn out onto a lightly floured surface and knead, using your hands and knuckles, until you have a soft, smooth, and elastic dough. If the dough feels too sticky, add a little flour, and if it fails to come together properly, add a little water. Alternatively, knead the dough in a freestanding tabletop mixer for 5 minutes.

Roll dough out to a thick circle. Spread raisins and walnuts over dough and carefully knead them in. Shape dough into a ball and put it into a greased bowl, turning it so that all the dough is greased. Cover and leave until doubled.

Turn dough out onto a lightly floured surface and knock back. Knead again and roll out to an 8x12-inch oblong, 3/8 inch thick. Brush dough with melted butter and sprinkle evenly with cinnamon sugar. Roll dough very tightly like a jelly roll, and pull it out at the corners as it shrinks a little. When you have finished rolling, seal edges by pinching them together.

Place roll, seam-side down, in the buttered bread pan, cover, and let rise again until doubled. Meanwhile, preheat the oven to 350°F. Remove cover, brush with a glaze of beaten egg and milk, and bake for about 40 minutes. Let cool for 10 minutes in the pan before turning out to cool completely on a wire rack.

Makes 1 loaf

brioches

see variations page 113

Brioche is a slightly sweet French bread, highly enriched with butter and eggs. You will need 12 x 3-inch fluted brioche pans for these little individual rolls.

2 cups bread flour
1/2 level tsp. salt
1 tbsp. sugar
3 tbsp. warm water (110°F)

1 envelope dry yeast
2 eggs, beaten, plus extra for brushing
2 tbsp. butter, melted
oil, for brushing

Sift flour and salt into a bowl. Dissolve sugar in warm water and sprinkle yeast on top. Leave for a few minutes until frothy, then stir it, together with beaten eggs and melted butter, into flour and salt. Using a wooden spoon, beat dough until it leaves the sides of the bowl clean, then turn it out onto a lightly floured surface and knead for 5 minutes. Alternatively, knead dough for 5 minutes in a freestanding tabletop mixer. Put dough in an oiled bowl, turn it around, cover with plastic wrap, and leave at room temperature to rise until doubled. Turn dough out onto a lightly floured surface and knead until smooth. Shape dough into a long sausage and cut into 12 equal pieces.

Brush brioche pans with oil and shape 3/4 of each piece of dough into a ball. Place it in a pan. Using a floured finger, press a hole in the center of the dough as far as the base of the pan. Shape remaining piece of dough into a ball and insert it in the hole. Press lightly with fingertip to unite the two pieces of dough. When all 12 brioches have been shaped, set pans on a cookie sheet, cover loosely with plastic wrap, and let rise until the dough is puffy and just below the tops of the pans. Preheat the oven to 450°F. Remove plastic wrap, brush the tops of the brioches with beaten egg, and bake for 10 minutes, or until golden brown.
Makes 12

all-day breakfast bread

see variations page 114

Some of your favorite breakfast ingredients wrapped up in a warm loaf of bread.

butter, for greasing
1 tsp. sugar
1 1/4 cups warm water (110°F)
1 envelope dry yeast
4 cups white bread flour
1 tsp. salt

for the filling
1 tbsp. butter, melted
4 strips cooked, crisp bacon
4 cooked sausage links, sliced
2 hard-boiled eggs, chopped

Grease a 2-lb. bread pan with butter. Dissolve sugar in warm water and sprinkle yeast on top. Leave until frothy, about 10-15 minutes. In a large bowl, mix flour and salt. Make a well in the center and pour in yeast liquid. Work to a soft dough. Turn out onto a lightly floured surface and knead with your hands and knuckles until the dough is soft, smooth, and elastic. Alternatively, knead dough in a freestanding tabletop mixer. Put dough into a greased bowl, turning it so that it is greased all over, cover, and let rise at room temperature until doubled in size.

Turn the dough out onto a lightly floured surface and roll out to an 8x12-inch rectangle. For the filling, brush with melted butter, then sprinkle bacon, sausage, and eggs evenly over top. Roll dough up like a jelly roll, and seal the edges together by pinching with your fingers. Put dough into greased bread pan, seam-side down, cover, and let rise until doubled.

Meanwhile, preheat oven to 425°F. Remove the cover and bake bread for about 30 minutes. Let cool in pan for 10 minutes, then turn out and cool on a wire rack.

Makes 1 loaf

banana cranberry loaf

see variations page 115

Slightly sweet and flavored with cranberries, this quick loaf is terrific toasted with butter.

6 tbsp. softened unsalted butter, plus extra
   for greasing
1/2 cup superfine sugar
1 1/2 cups all-purpose flour
1/4 cup whole wheat flour
1/2 tsp. salt

2 tsp. baking powder
1/4 tsp. baking soda
3 medium-size bananas (2 very ripe)
1/4 cup buttermilk
2 large eggs, beaten
1/2 cup chopped dried cranberries

Preheat the oven to 350°F. Grease a 1-pound loaf pan and dust with flour. In a large bowl, beat the butter and the sugar together until creamy. In a separate bowl, combine the dry ingredients. In yet another bowl, mash the 2 ripe bananas with the buttermilk.

Add the beaten eggs gradually to the creamed butter and sugar. Add the mashed bananas and the dry ingredients and mix lightly until combined. Do not overmix. Slice the third banana and add it to the batter with the cranberries, stirring lightly until just combined. Pour the batter into the loaf pan and bake in the middle of the oven for about 40 minutes or until a toothpick inserted into the center comes out clean. Leave in the pan for 10 minutes, then turn out and cool on a wire rack.

Makes 1 loaf

monkey bread

see variations page 116

This is a sweet pull-apart bread, delicious when at room temperature, delectable when warm. Traditionally monkey bread is baked in a tube pan, but a round dish is fine.

butter, for greasing
1 tsp. sugar
1 1/4 cups warm milk (110°F)
1 envelope dry yeast
4 cups white bread flour
1 tsp. salt
1 tbsp. grated orange zest

for glaze & coating
5 tbsp. butter, melted
3 tbsp. orange juice
1/4 cup brown sugar
1 1/2 cups sugar
1 tbsp. ground cinnamon

Grease a large tube pan, round casserole dish, or cake pan. Dissolve sugar in warm milk, then sprinkle yeast over top. Set aside until frothy, 10-15 minutes. In a large bowl, mix flour, salt, and orange zest. Make a well in the center and pour in yeast liquid. Work to a soft dough, turn out onto a lightly floured surface, and knead until it is soft, smooth, and elastic (or use a mixer). Place dough in a greased bowl, turning to grease all over, cover, and let rise in a warm place until doubled in size.

To make glaze, in a small pan, mix melted butter with orange juice, then add brown sugar and stir to dissolve. In a small bowl, mix cinnamon and sugar. Turn dough onto a lightly floured surface, knock back, and break into about 30–35 pieces. Roll into balls. Dip each ball into the glaze and then roll in the cinnamon sugar. Start layering the balls in the tube pan, leaving room on the bottom layer for the balls to expand as they rise. They should be close, but not touching. On each successive layer, place balls so that they overlap empty spaces

underneath. When you have used up all the balls, cover and let rise until doubled in size. Meanwhile, preheat the oven to 350°F. Remove cover from bread, pour any remaining glaze over the top, and sprinkle on remaining cinnamon sugar. Bake for about 25-30 minutes, until lightly browned. Invert bread onto a serving plate, being careful of hot syrup. Cool slightly, then serve.

Makes 1

classic french baguette

see variations page 117

This bread will become stale within one day, so it's best eaten as soon as possible.

1 tsp. sugar	3 cups white bread flour
1 cup warm water (110°F)	1 tsp. salt
1 envelope dry yeast	

Dissolve the sugar in the warm water, then sprinkle the yeast on top. Leave until frothy, about 10-15 minutes. In a large bowl, mix flour and salt. Make a well in the center, pour in yeast liquid, and work to a soft dough. Turn onto a lightly floured surface and knead until you have a soft, smooth, and elastic dough. Alternatively, knead in a freestanding tabletop mixer for 5 minutes. Place dough in a greased bowl, turning it so that it is greased all over, cover, and let rise at room temperature until doubled.

Turn dough out onto a lightly floured surface and knock back lightly. Roll out to a 16x12-inch rectangle, and then cut in half to make two 8x12-inch rectangles. Roll up each piece tightly from the longer side, pounding any air bubbles as you go. Pinch together the dough along the seam and at each end. Place seam-side down, 3 inches apart, on a greased cookie sheet and make deep gashes diagonally across each loaf every 2 inches. Cover and let rise until doubled in size.

Meanwhile, preheat the oven to 425°F. Remove cover from the loaves and bake for 10-12 minutes or until golden brown. Cool on a wire rack.

Makes 2 loaves

variations

rustic loaf

see base recipe page 85

tomato & olive loaf
Prepare basic recipe, adding 1/2 cup pitted and chopped black olives and
1/4 cup drained and chopped sun-dried tomatoes during the first kneading.

apple bran bread
Prepare basic recipe, replacing 1/4 cup bread flour with 1/4 cup whole wheat
flour. Add 1 tablespoon wheat bran; 2 apples, peeled, cored, and shredded;
1 tablespoon sugar; and 1 teaspoon ground cinnamon.

basil & parmesan loaf
Prepare basic recipe, adding 1 tablespoon dried basil and 2 tablespoons
finely shredded Parmesan cheese to the flour.

foccacia
Prepare basic recipe. After the first rising, roll dough into a round about
1/2 inch thick. Place on cookie sheet and sprinkle with 2 teaspoons dried
rosemary and 2 minced garlic cloves. Poke shallow indentations all over
dough with your fingertips, then pour 1 tablespoon olive oil on top so it
pools in indentations. Bake for about 20 minutes, until lightly browned.

variations

no-yeast soda bread

see base recipe page 86

soda bread with onion & dill
Prepare the basic recipe, adding 1 tablespoon dry minced onion and
1 tablespoon dried dill to the flour before mixing.

soda bread with cheese & mustard
Prepare the basic recipe, adding 1/2 cup shredded Cheddar cheese and
2 teaspoons dry mustard to the flour before mixing.

soda bread with sweet red bell pepper & sage
Prepare the basic recipe, adding 1/4 cup finely chopped roasted sweet red
bell peppers and 1 tablespoon (or less, if desired) dried sage to the flour
before mixing.

soda bread with fruit & oats
Prepare the basic recipe, replacing 2 tablespoons of the flour with 2 tablespoons
rolled oats and adding 1/2 cup chopped dried fruit and 1 tablespoon
ground cinnamon.

variations

multigrain bread

see base recipe page 89

multigrain bread with brown sugar & pecans
Prepare the basic recipe, omitting the honey. Add 4 tablespoons brown sugar and 1/4 cup chopped pecans to the flours before mixing.

multigrain bread with bulgur wheat
Prepare the basic recipe, adding 3 tablespoons bulgur wheat to the flours before mixing.

multigrain & orange bread
Prepare the basic recipe, replacing the milk with buttermilk. Add 2 tablespoons grated orange zest to the flours before mixing.

multigrain bread with garlic & rosemary
Prepare the basic recipe, omitting the honey. Add 1 minced garlic clove and 1 tablespoon dried rosemary to the flours before mixing.

multigrain bread with sunflower seeds
Prepare the basic recipe, adding 3 tablespoons sunflower seeds to the flours before mixing.

variations

raisin bread

see base recipe page 90

raisin bread with coconut & banana
Prepare the basic recipe, adding 1/4 cup unsweetened shredded coconut and
1 mashed banana.

raisin bread with mango & macadamia nuts
Prepare the basic recipe, omitting 1/4 cup raisins and adding 1/4 cup chopped
fresh mango and 1/4 cup chopped macadamia nuts.

raisin bread with orange & almond
Prepare the basic recipe, omitting 1/4 cup raisins and adding 1 tablespoon finely
chopped orange zest and 1/4 cup chopped almonds.

cranberry–raisin bread
Prepare the basic recipe, replacing 1/4 cup raisins with 1/4 cup dried cranberries.

cherry–raisin bread
Prepare the basic recipe, replacing 1/4 cup raisins with 1/4 cup dried cherries.

variations

brötchen

see base recipe page 92

poppy seed brötchen
Prepare the basic recipe, adding 2 tablespoons poppy seeds.

brötchen with flaxseeds
Prepare the basic recipe, omitting 1/4 cup white bread flour, and substituting 1/4 cup flaxseed meal and 2 teaspoons malt powder (if available). Sprinkle a few flaxseeds on top of the rolls before baking, pressing them into the dough slightly.

brötchen with whole wheat flour
Prepare the basic recipe, replacing 1 1/4 cups white bread flour with 1 1/4 cups whole wheat flour.

brötchen with bran & sesame seeds
Prepare the basic recipe, omitting 1/4 cup white bread flour and adding 2 tablespoons wheat bran and 2 tablespoons sesame seeds.

brötchen with garlic pepper
Prepare the basic recipe, adding 1 finely chopped garlic clove and 1 tablespoon garlic pepper to the flour before mixing.

variations

italian herb bread

see base recipe page 93

italian herb bread with lemon & poppy seed
Prepare the basic recipe, omitting the oil, garlic, and herbs. Add 1 tablespoon grated lemon zest and 1 tablespoon poppy seeds.

italian herb bread with pesto swirl
Prepare the basic recipe, omitting the herbs. After the first rising, roll the dough out to an 8x14-inch rectangle. Spread 4 tablespoons pesto over the dough and roll it up like a jelly roll. Put into a greased baking pan for the second rising until doubled in size. Bake for about 30 minutes.

italian cardamom & herb bread
Prepare the basic recipe, adding 2 teaspoons ground cardamom to the other herbs.

italian herb bread with onion & oregano
Prepare the basic recipe, omitting the thyme and adding 1 tablespoon dried onion flakes and an extra 2 teaspoons oregano.

italian herb bread with pumpkin seeds
Prepare the basic recipe, omitting the garlic and adding 1/4 cup pumpkin seeds.

variations

pumpkin swirl bread

see base recipe page 94

pumpkin swirl bread with trail mix
Prepare the basic recipe, replacing the cinnamon sugar in the swirl with
3 tablespoons trail mix.

pumpkin, cranberry & orange swirl bread
Prepare the basic recipe, replacing the raisins with 1/2 cup dried cranberries
and 1 tablespoons grated orange zest.

pumpkin, apple & ginger swirl bread
Prepare the basic recipe, replacing the raisins with 2 peeled, cored, and finely
shredded apples. Add an extra teaspoon of ground ginger to the ingredients.

pumpkin, pecan & golden raisin swirl bread
Prepare the basic recipe, replacing the raisins and walnuts with golden
raisins and chopped pecans.

pumpkin, cherry & almond swirl bread
Prepare the basic recipe, replacing the raisins and walnuts with dried cherries
and chopped almonds.

variations

brioches

see base recipe page 97

brioches with raisins
Prepare the basic recipe, adding 1/2 cup raisins to the flour with the water and butter.

brioches with chocolate
Prepare the basic recipe, adding 1/2 cup semisweet chocolate chips to the flour with the water and butter.

brioches with cinnamon
Prepare the basic recipe, adding 2 teaspoons ground cinnamon to the flour before stirring in yeast mixture.

brioches with nutmeg
Prepare the basic recipe, adding 1 teaspoon ground nutmeg to the flour before stirring in yeast mixture.

brioches with almonds
Prepare the basic recipe. After brushing the brioches with beaten egg, scatter a few sliced almonds over the top of each one.

variations

all-day breakfast bread

see base recipe page 98

maple & pecan breakfast bread
Prepare the basic recipe, omitting the bacon, sausage, and eggs. Add
2 tablespoons melted butter and 2 tablespoons maple syrup to the flour
mixture. Sprinkle 1/2 cup chopped pecans and 1/4 cup brown sugar on the
dough before rolling up.

cheese & black olive breakfast bread
Prepare the basic recipe, omitting the bacon, sausage, and eggs.
Substitute 1/4 cup pitted and chopped black olives and 1/2 cup
shredded Cheddar cheese.

ham & mushroom breakfast bread
Prepare the basic recipe, omitting the bacon, sausage and eggs. Substitute
1/2 cup chopped ham and 1/4 cup chopped lightly fried mushrooms.

cheese & onion breakfast bread
Prepare the basic recipe, omitting the sausage and eggs. Substitute 1/4 cup
shredded Cheddar cheese and 1/4 cup chopped lightly fried onion.

variations

banana cranberry loaf

see base recipe page 101

banana, cherry & macadamia loaf
Prepare the basic recipe, omitting the cranberries and substituting 1/4 cup chopped glacé cherries and 1/4 cup chopped macadamia nuts.

banana, fig & almond loaf
Prepare the basic recipe, omitting the cranberries and substituting 1/4 cup chopped dried figs and 1/4 cup chopped almonds.

banana, date & walnut loaf
Prepare the basic recipe, omitting the cranberries and substituting 1/4 cup chopped dates and 1/4 cup chopped walnuts.

tropical pineapple & coconut loaf
Prepare the basic recipe, omitting the cranberries and substituting 1/4 cup chopped candied pineapple and 1/4 cup unsweetened shredded coconut.

banana cranberry loaf with ginger
Prepare the basic recipe, adding 2 teaspoons ground ginger.

variations

monkey bread

see base recipe page 102

monkey bread with maple cinnamon sugar
Prepare the basic recipe, omitting the orange zest and orange juice, and
1/4 cup of the white sugar, and substituting 3 tablespoons maple syrup.

monkey bread with garlic & herbs
Prepare the basic recipe, replacing orange zest with 1 pressed garlic clove. Omit
orange juice, both sugars, and cinnamon in the glaze. Instead, mix melted
butter with 2 pressed garlic cloves and 1/2 teaspoon each of dried sage,
rosemary, and basil.

monkey bread with apples & brown sugar
Prepare the basic recipe. In a plastic bag, shake 1 tablespoon ground cinnamon
with 1/2 cup brown sugar. Add 2 peeled and sliced apples, shake to coat, and
layer in pan with dough balls.

bananas foster monkey bread
Prepare the basic recipe. In a plastic bag, shake 1 tablespoon cinnamon with
1/2 cup brown sugar. Add 2 coarsely chopped bananas, shake to coat, and layer
in pan with dough balls.

classic french baguette

see base recipe page 105

french baguette with chile & cheese
Prepare the basic recipe. Add 2 teaspoons crushed dried chile flakes (or to taste) and 2 tablespoons finely grated Parmesan cheese to the flour before mixing. Just before baking, brush with a little melted butter and sprinkle with a little finely grated Parmesan cheese.

french baguette with garlic & thyme
Prepare the basic recipe. Add 2 garlic cloves, pressed, and 2 teaspoons dried thyme to the flour before mixing. Brush with a little garlic oil just before baking.

french baguette with oregano & poppy seed
Prepare the basic recipe. Add 2 teaspoons dried oregano and 1 tablespoon poppy seeds to the flour before mixing.

french baguette with dill & sesame seed
Prepare the basic recipe. Add 2 teaspoons dried dill and 1 tablespoon sesame seeds to the flour before mixing. Brush with melted butter and a little dried dill just before baking.

pastries &
muffins

From time-consuming but impressive buttery

croissants to quick, fruity, and savory muffins, this

chapter has something for everyone.

fresh-from-the-oven pop tarts

see variations page 142

These are far superior to store-bought and quite simple to make. You can make them the day before and chill in fridge overnight.

2 cups flour
1 tbsp. sugar
1 tsp. salt
1 cup unsalted butter, very cold and cubed
1 egg, beaten
2 tbsp. cold milk (or less)

for the filling & glaze
1/2 cup brown sugar
1 1/2 tsp. ground cinnamon
4 tsp. flour
1 egg, beaten

In a large bowl, mix flour, sugar, and salt. Using a pastry blender, cut in butter until it resembles coarse breadcrumbs. Add beaten egg and enough milk to just bring the dough together. Divide dough in half, wrap each piece in plastic wrap, and chill for 30 minutes. Remove dough from fridge and allow to soften a little, about 10 minutes. Remove plastic wrap and roll each piece out on a lightly floured surface until each is a 10x12-inch rectangle. Trim edges. Cut each piece into 9 smaller (3x5-inch) rectangles. To make the filling, mix brown sugar, cinnamon, and flour. Take 1 pastry rectangle, brush with beaten egg, then sprinkle a little of the filling in the middle, leaving a generous margin all around. Place another rectangle exactly on top and seal edges together with your fingers. Press with tines of a fork to seal completely, and then prick a few times to allow steam to escape during cooking. Repeat with the remaining pastry rectangles. Carefully place tarts on a greased, lined cookie sheet and brush with beaten egg to glaze. Refrigerate for 30 minutes (or overnight, if you wish). Preheat oven to 350°F. Remove tarts from fridge and bake for 25-35 minutes until light golden brown. Allow to cool before removing from cookie sheet.

Makes 9

cherry kuchen

see variations page 143

Kuchen is the German word for cake. This recipe is so quick to put together, you can have it on the table in 45 minutes.

1 cup (2 sticks) unsalted butter, softened
1 cup sugar
2 large eggs
2 cups flour
2 tsp. baking powder

1 tsp. vanilla extract
a little milk, if needed
1 (16-oz.) can cherry pie filling
1/3 cup sliced almonds
powdered sugar, to dust

Preheat the oven to 350°F and grease a 9x11-inch baking pan. Mix the first six ingredients together to make a batter. If the batter is too thick, thin it with a little milk. Pour most of the batter into the bottom of the greased baking pan.

Pour the can of cherry pie filling on top and drop the remaining batter on top of the cherries. Scatter some sliced almonds on top. Bake for 35-40 minutes. Cool, then dust with powdered sugar.

Serves 12

blueberry & white chocolate muffins

see variations page 144

The trick to making perfect muffins is to combine the wet ingredients from one bowl into the dry ingredients in another bowl as lightly and quickly as possible.

2 1/4 cups flour
1 tbsp. baking powder
pinch salt
1/2 cup sugar
1 cup white chocolate chips (or chopped white chocolate)

1 cup fresh blueberries
2 large eggs
6 tbsp. unsalted butter, melted
1 1/8 cups buttermilk
1 tsp. vanilla extract

Preheat the oven to 400°F and line a 12-cup muffin pan with paper muffin cups. In a bowl, sift together the flour, baking powder, and salt. Stir in the sugar, white chocolate, and blueberries. In another bowl, whisk the eggs, then whisk in the melted butter, buttermilk, and vanilla extract.

Make a well in the center of the dry ingredients and quickly pour in the wet ingredients. Stir quickly and lightly until just combined. It does not matter if there are a few lumps and dry bits. Spoon quickly into the muffin cups and bake for 20-25 minutes until golden, firm to the touch, and well risen. Serve warm or cool on a wire rack.

Makes 12

danish pastries

see variations page 145

Baking with yeast can be very satisfying, especially when the end result is as delicious as these. You can start them the day before and let them rise in the refrigerator overnight.

4 tsp. sugar
1/3 cup warm water (110°F)
1 envelope dry yeast
2 cups all-purpose flour
1 tsp. salt
1 tbsp. vegetable shortening
1 large egg, lightly beaten

1/2 cup (1 stick) unsalted butter
1 cup almond paste
for the top
1 egg, beaten
3/4 cup powdered sugar
1 tbsp. milk

Dissolve 1 teaspoon sugar in warm water, then sprinkle yeast on top. Leave until frothy, 10-15 minutes. In a large bowl, mix flour with salt, then, using a pastry blender or your fingertips, cut in shortening until mixture resembles fine breadcrumbs. Make a well in the center and pour in yeast liquid, beaten egg, and remaining sugar. Mix to a soft dough. Knead until dough is soft, smooth, and elastic, using your fingers and knuckles. Alternatively, knead in a freestanding tabletop mixer for 5 minutes. Cover and leave in a cool place for 10 minutes.

Work the butter until it is a 9x3-inch block. Roll out dough to a 10-inch square and place butter block in the center. Fold the dough sides up over it. Roll out dough to a 15x5-inch oblong. Fold top third down and bottom third up. Put in a greased plastic bag and let rest for 20 minutes in the fridge. Repeat this process twice, finally resting for 40 minutes. At this stage you can rest the dough overnight in the fridge.

Roll out half the dough to a 10-inch square, then cut it into four equal pieces. Fold two corners of each square to meet in the center, like an envelope, and repeat with the other two corners. Press down firmly to seal. Place a small round of almond paste in the center. Repeat with the remaining dough. Set pastries well apart on greased cookie sheets and cover loosely with plastic wrap. Let rise in a warm place for 20 minutes.

Heat the oven to 425°F. Remove plastic wrap and brush the pastries with lightly beaten egg. Bake for about 10 minutes, until golden brown. Mix the powdered sugar and milk to make the glaze, and brush it over the pastries while they are still warm. Cool on a wire rack, or serve warm.

Makes 8

crumble-topped cheese muffins

see variations page 146

Not everyone likes sweet muffins for breakfast. These savory muffins have the benefit of protein as well.

2 1/4 cups flour
1 tbsp. baking powder
pinch salt
freshly ground black pepper
1 cup shredded Cheddar cheese
1/2 cup chopped cooked ham
4 tbsp. snipped fresh chives
2 large eggs
1 1/8 cups buttermilk

6 tbsp. butter, melted
1 tsp. French mustard (a strong, dark mustard)

for the crumble topping
1/2 cup flour
1/4 cup (1/2 stick) cold butter
1/4 cup shredded Cheddar cheese
salt and freshly ground black pepper

Preheat the oven to 400°F and line a 12-cup muffin pan with paper muffin cups. First make the crumble topping. Put the flour into a medium bowl and cut in the butter using a pastry blender or your fingertips until the mixture resembles fine bread crumbs. Stir in the shredded cheese and season with salt and pepper. Set aside.

In a large bowl, sift together the flour, baking powder, and salt and pepper to taste. Add the shredded cheese, chopped ham, and chives. In another bowl, whisk the eggs, then whisk in the buttermilk, melted butter, and mustard. Make a well in the center of the dry ingredients and quickly pour in the wet ingredients. Fold gently until just combined; do not overmix. Quickly spoon batter into the muffin cups and sprinkle with the crumble topping. Bake for 20 minutes until golden brown, well risen, and firm to the touch. Serve warm or cool on a wire rack.

Makes 12

jelly doughnut muffins

see variations page 147

The sugar sprinkled on the muffins, and the jelly inside, make these taste just like jelly doughnuts.

2 1/4 cups flour
1 tbsp. baking powder
pinch salt
1/2 cup granulated sugar
2 large eggs
3/4 cup plus 2 tbsp. milk
6 tbsp. butter, melted

1 tsp. vanilla extract
4 tbsp. good-quality strawberry jelly

for the topping
4 tbsp. butter, melted
1/2 cup sugar

Preheat the oven to 400°F and line a 12-cup muffin pan with paper muffin cups. In a large bowl, sift the flour, baking powder, and salt together. Add the sugar and stir to combine. In another bowl, whisk the eggs, then whisk in the milk, melted butter, and vanilla extract. Make a well in the center of the dry ingredients and quickly pour in the wet ingredients. Stir very gently until just combined; do not overmix. Spoon half the batter into the prepared muffin cups. Add a teaspoon of jelly to the center of each muffin, and then spoon in the rest of the batter. Bake for about 20 minutes until well risen, golden brown, and firm to the touch.

Prepare the topping while the muffins are cooking. Place the melted butter and sugar separately in two wide, shallow dishes. Cool the muffins for 5 minutes, then dip the top of each muffin in the melted butter and then dip in the sugar. Serve warm or cool on a wire rack.

Makes 12

pumpkin & pecan muffins

see variations page 148

These are moist and flavored with fall spices.

2 1/4 cups flour
1 tbsp. baking powder
1/2 tsp. baking soda
pinch salt
2/3 cup brown sugar
3/4 cup chopped pecans
1 tsp. ground cinnamon
1 tsp. pumpkin pie spice

2 large eggs
1 cup sour cream
6 tbsp. butter, melted
1 tsp. vanilla extract
3/4 cup canned pumpkin
12 pecan halves
3 tbsp. maple syrup, to glaze

Preheat the oven to 400°F and line a 12-cup muffin pan with paper muffin cups. In a large bowl, sift the flour, baking powder, baking soda, and salt together. Add the brown sugar, chopped pecans, cinnamon, and pumpkin pie spice. Stir to combine. In another bowl, whisk the eggs, then whisk in the sour cream, melted butter, vanilla extract, and pumpkin.
Make a well in the center of the dry ingredients and quickly pour in the wet ingredients, stirring quickly and gently until just combined. Spoon into the muffin cups and top each muffin with a pecan half. Bake for about 20 minutes until golden brown, well risen, and firm to the touch.

Cool the muffins in the pan for 5 minutes, then brush them with the maple syrup to glaze. Serve warm or cool on a wire rack.

Makes 12

whole wheat muesli &
sunflower seed muffins

see variations page 149

The sunflower seeds add a wonderful crunch to these muffins, and the sunflower oil is healthier than butter.

1 cup all-purpose flour
1/2 cup whole wheat flour
1 tbsp. baking powder
pinch salt
1/4 cup rolled oats
2 tbsp. wheat bran
1/2 cup raisins

2/3 cup brown sugar
1/2 cup sunflower seeds
2 large eggs
1 1/8 cups buttermilk
6 tbsp. sunflower oil (or substitute canola oil)
1 tsp. vanilla extract

Preheat the oven to 400°F and line a 12-cup muffin pan with paper muffin cups. In a large bowl, sift together the flours, baking powder, and salt. Stir in the rolled oats, wheat bran, raisins, brown sugar, and sunflower seeds. In another bowl, whisk the eggs, then whisk in the buttermilk, sunflower oil, and vanilla extract.

Make a well in the center of the dry ingredients and quickly pour in the wet ingredients. Stir gently until just combined; do not overmix. Spoon batter into the muffin cups and bake for about 20 minutes until well risen, golden brown, and firm to the touch. Serve warm or cool on a wire rack.

Makes 12

banana, cranberry & walnut muffins

see variations page 150

Bananas make a wonderful addition to muffins because they add a delicious moistness.

2 cups all-purpose flour
1/4 cup whole wheat flour
1 tbsp. baking powder
1/2 tsp. salt
2 tbsp. rolled oats
2/3 cup brown sugar
3/4 cup chopped walnuts
1/2 cup dried cranberries
2 large bananas

2 large eggs, lightly beaten
1 cup buttermilk
6 tbsp. sunflower or canola oil
1 tsp. vanilla extract

for topping
3 tbsp. apricot preserves
1/2 cup chopped walnuts

Preheat the oven to 400°F and line a 12-cup muffin pan with paper muffin cups. In a large bowl, sift together the flours, baking powder, and salt. Stir in the rolled oats, brown sugar, walnuts, and cranberries. In another bowl, mash the bananas, then stir in the beaten eggs, buttermilk, oil, and vanilla extract.

Make a well in the center of the dry ingredients and quickly pour in the wet ingredients, stirring gently until just combined. Do not overmix. Spoon into the muffin cups and bake for about 20 minutes until well risen, golden brown, and firm to the touch. Let cool in the pan for 5 minutes. Gently heat the jelly and brush it on top of the muffins, then sprinkle with the walnuts. Serve warm or cool on a wire rack.

Makes 12

heart-friendly muffins

see variations page 151

Though low in saturated fat, these are absolutely delicious. They're best eaten within a day of baking.

1 3/4 cups all-purpose flour
1/4 cup whole wheat flour
1 tbsp. baking powder
zest of 1 lemon
1/2 cup granulated sugar
1/3 cup brown sugar
1 banana
1 egg, beaten

1 1/4 cups buttermilk
5 tbsp. canola oil
1 cup blueberries

for glaze
2 tsp. freshly squeezed lemon juice
1 tbsp. granulated sugar

Preheat the oven to 400°F and line a 12-cup muffin pan with paper muffin cups. In a large bowl, sift together the flours and baking powder. Stir in the lemon zest and the sugars. In another bowl, mash the banana, then stir in the beaten egg, buttermilk, and oil.

Make a well in the center of the dry ingredients, then quickly pour in the wet ingredients, stirring gently until just combined. Do not overmix. Add the blueberries and give just a few turns to combine them without crushing them.

Spoon the mixture into the muffin cups and bake for about 20 minutes until well risen, golden brown, and firm to the touch. While the muffins are cooling for 5 minutes, mix the sugar and lemon juice together and brush over the muffins to glaze them while they are still warm. Serve warm or cool on a wire rack.

Makes 12

parmesan & pine nut muffins

see variations page 152

With their hint of garlic, these savory muffins will fill your kitchen with a wonderful aroma.

2 1/4 cups flour
1 tbsp. baking powder
pinch salt
freshly ground black pepper to taste
1/3 cup finely shredded Parmesan cheese
1/2 cup pine nuts
1 tsp. garlic powder
1 tbsp. dried Italian herbs

2 large eggs
1 tsp. French mustard
1 1/8 cups buttermilk
6 tbsp. sunflower oil

for topping
2 tbsp. finely shredded Parmesan cheese
2 tbsp. pine nuts

Preheat the oven to 400°F and line a 12-cup muffin pan with paper muffin cups. In a large bowl, sift together the flour, baking powder, and salt. Add the black pepper, the Parmesan cheese, pine nuts, garlic powder, and herbs. Stir until combined. In another bowl, whisk the eggs, then whisk in the mustard, buttermilk, and sunflower oil.

Make a well in the center of the dry ingredients, then quickly pour in the wet ingredients, stirring gently until just combined. Do not overmix. Spoon batter into the muffin cups, then sprinkle on the Parmesan cheese and pine nuts for the topping. Bake for about 20 minutes until well risen, golden brown, and firm to the touch. Cool in the pan for 5 minutes, then serve warm.

Makes 12

flaky croissants

see variations page 153

Although a simplified version, these are still quite time-consuming, so start them the day before and refrigerate overnight. In the morning, bring them back to room temperature and let rise until doubled in size, an hour or so, before baking. These also freeze well. Freeze, uncovered, immediately upon forming into crescents. Cover once frozen. Defrost overnight, then let rise until doubled.

1 cup warm milk (110°F)	4 cups white bread flour
1/4 cup plus 1 tsp. sugar	1 tsp. salt
1 envelope dry yeast	1 cup (2 sticks) butter, very cold
1 cup all-purpose or white bread flour	1 tsp. sugar
1 egg, beaten	2 tsp. water
1/2 cup (1 stick) butter, softened, not melted	1 egg, beaten

Stir the warm milk and 1 teaspoon sugar together. Add yeast, then set aside until frothy, about 10 minutes. Add flour and beat well. Add remaining sugar and egg, and beat again until smooth. Add butter, beat, and set aside. Put the 4 cups flour and salt into the bowl of a food processor. Add the 2 sticks butter, cut into small cubes, and pulse briefly until butter is the size of peas. The idea now is to get a soft dough without melting the pieces of butter, so it needs to stay really cold. Tip flour and butter mixture into a large bowl, add milk and yeast mixture, and mix until moistened. Cover bowl and refrigerate for 2 hours.

Remove from fridge, turn out onto a lightly floured surface, and knead lightly, then roll dough into a rectangle about 18x12 inches in size. Working as quickly as possible, fold the dough into thirds, bringing the bottom third up and folding the top third over. Put into a

greased plastic bag and back in the fridge for 1 hour. Repeat the rolling and chilling twice more. You can leave dough in the fridge overnight at this stage. Divide dough into four parts. Keep three parts chilled, and roll out the fourth into a circle about 12 inches across. Cut circle into six pie-shaped wedges. For each croissant, with your fingers roll each wedge from the wide edge toward the point, stretching the dough slightly as you roll. Curl them into crescents, place on floured cookie sheets, and cover loosely. Repeat with remaining dough. Let crescents rise at room temperature until doubled in size. This could take 2 hours. Preheat oven to 400°F. Make egg wash by mixing the sugar and water, then adding the egg. Remove cover from croissants, brush with egg wash, and put into the oven. Immediately turn temperature down to 350°F and bake for 15-20 minutes until golden.

Makes 24

variations

fresh-from-the-oven pop tarts

see base recipe page 119

berry pop tarts
Prepare the basic recipe. Replace the filling and beaten egg with 2 teaspoons good-quality berry jelly (strawberry or raspberry both work well) per tart. After baking, glaze with a little powdered sugar mixed with a little water.

chocolate chip pop tarts
Prepare the basic recipe. Replace the filling and beaten egg with 2 teaspoons semisweet chocolate chips per tart. After baking, glaze with a little powdered sugar mixed with a little water.

apple strudel pop tarts
Prepare the basic recipe. Replace the filling with a mixture of 2 teaspoons canned apple pie filling and a few golden raisins and a little ground cinnamon to spread on each tart.

apricot & almond pop tarts
Prepare the basic recipe, omitting the filling and beaten egg. Substitute 2 teaspoons good-quality apricot jelly for each one. Sprinkle with some sliced almonds. After baking, glaze with a little powdered sugar mixed with a little water.

cherry kuchen

see base recipe page 120

apricot & almond kuchen
Prepare the basic recipe, adding 1 teaspoon almond extract to the batter.
Instead of the cherry filling, drain 1 (16-ounce) can apricots. Heat juice with
2 tablespoons cornstarch and 2 tablespoons orange juice until boiling and
thickened. Chop apricots, add to the pan, and cool before using.

apple & cinnamon kuchen
Prepare the basic recipe, replacing the butter with 1 cup canola oil. Instead of
the cherry filling, stew 2 peeled and sliced apples with 2 tablespoons sugar and
2 teaspoons cinnamon. Cool before using.

plum kuchen
Prepare the basic recipe, omitting the cherries. Substitute 2 cups pitted and
chopped plums, stewed gently in a little water and a little sugar to taste. Cool
before using.

rhubarb & orange kuchen
Prepare the basic recipe, omitting the cherries. Substitute 2 cups sliced rhubarb,
stewed in a little orange juice and sugar to taste. Thicken with cornstarch if
needed. Cool before using.

variations

blueberry & white chocolate muffins

see base recipe page 123

cherry, coconut & white chocolate muffins
Prepare the basic recipe, omitting the blueberries and 1/4 cup of white chocolate. Add 1/4 cup unsweetened shredded coconut and 1 cup pitted and chopped fresh cherries.

blueberry & chocolate muffins
Prepare the basic recipe, replacing the white chocolate chips with semisweet chocolate chips.

raspberry & white chocolate muffins
Prepare the basic recipe, replacing the blueberries with 1 cup coarsely chopped fresh raspberries.

double chocolate blueberry muffins
Prepare the basic recipe, replacing 1/4 cup white chocolate chips with 1/4 cup semisweet chocolate chips.

blueberry fruit explosion muffins
Prepare the basic recipe, replacing the white chocolate chips with 1/4 cup each dried cherries, cranberries, raisins, and chopped dried dates.

danish pastries

see base recipe page 124

pecan pinwheels

Prepare basic recipe. Cut each pastry square almost to the middle from each corner. Make a filling with 3/4 cup ground pecans, 1 tablespoon maple syrup, and 1/3 cup brown sugar. Place 1 teaspoon filling in middle of each square and fold in each point of pastry. Continue with the basic recipe, adding some chopped pecans mixed with a little sugar on top of the egg wash before baking.

danish pastries with apricot

Prepare basic recipe. Place 2 teaspoons custard in middle of each square. Top with 2 canned apricot halves and dot with apricot jelly. Fold 2 corners into middle and pinch to seal. Continue with basic recipe.

danish pastries with strawberry

Prepare basic recipe. Place 2 teaspoons custard in middle of each square. Top with strawberries and dot with strawberry jelly. Fold 2 corners into middle and pinch to seal. Continue with basic recipe.

raisin whirls

Prepare basic recipe, but roll pastry into a rectangle. Make a filling with 1/3 cup raisins, 1/4 cup sugar, 1/4 cup soft butter, and 1 teaspoon pumpkin pie spice. Spread over dough, roll up like a jelly roll, cut into slices, and press each one down on cookie sheet. Continue with basic recipe.

variations

crumble-topped ham & cheese muffins

see base recipe page 126

crumble-topped rosemary, ham & cheese muffins
Prepare the basic recipe, omitting the chopped chives and substituting 4 teaspoons chopped dried rosemary.

crumble-topped sausage & cheese muffins
Prepare the basic recipe, replacing the ham and chives with 1/2 cup chopped, cooked, spicy sausage and 2 tablespoons dried sage.

crumble-topped zucchini & cheese muffins
Prepare the basic recipe, replacing the ham and chives with 1/2 cup chopped, cooked zucchini and 2 tablespoons dried oregano.

crumble-topped spinach & nutmeg muffins
Prepare the basic recipe, replacing the ham and chives with 1/2 cup chopped, cooked spinach and 2 teaspoons ground nutmeg.

crumble-topped carrot & cilantro muffins
Prepare the basic recipe, replacing the ham and chives with 1/2 cup grated peeled carrots and 2 tablespoons freshly chopped cilantro.

variations

jelly doughnut muffins

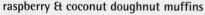

see base recipe page 129

raspberry & coconut doughnut muffins
Prepare the basic recipe, adding 1/4 cup unsweetened shredded coconut
to the batter. Replace the strawberry jelly with raspberry jelly.

apricot & almond doughnut muffins
Prepare the basic recipe, replacing the vanilla extract with almond extract
and the strawberry jelly with apricot jelly.

black cherry doughnut muffins
Prepare the basic recipe, replacing the strawberry jelly with black cherry jelly.

lemon & black currant doughnut muffins
Prepare the basic recipe, adding 2 teaspoons finely shredded lemon zest
to the muffin batter. Replace the strawberry jelly with black currant jelly.

orange doughnut muffins
Prepare the basic recipe, replacing the strawberry jelly with orange marmalade.

variations

pumpkin & pecan muffins

see base recipe page 130

butternut squash & walnut muffins
Prepare the basic recipe, replacing the canned pumpkin with 3/4 cup cooked butternut squash pulp and the pecans with 3/4 cup chopped walnuts. Top the muffins with walnut halves.

carrot & cilantro muffins
Prepare the basic recipe, replacing the canned pumpkin with 3/4 cup cooked and mashed carrots and the pumpkin pie spice with 2 tablespoons chopped fresh cilantro.

zucchini & chocolate chip muffins
Prepare the basic recipe, replacing the canned pumpkin with 3/4 cup cooked, chopped zucchini and the pecans with 1/2 cup semisweet chocolate chips.

pumpkin, pecan & raisin muffins
Prepare the basic recipe, adding 3/4 cup raisins to the batter.

pumpkin, fig & pistachio muffins
Prepare the basic recipe, replacing the pecans with 1/2 cup chopped dried figs and 1/4 cup shelled chopped pistachios.

whole wheat muesli & sunflower seed muffins

see base recipe page 133

whole wheat ginger & apple spice muffins
Prepare the basic recipe, omitting half the raisins and adding 1/4 cup chopped apple, 3 teaspoons ground ginger, 2 teaspoons ground cinnamon, and 2 teaspoons ground nutmeg.

whole wheat maple oatmeal muffins
Prepare the basic recipe, replacing 1/2 cup of the buttermilk with 1/2 cup maple syrup.

whole wheat peach muesli muffins
Prepare the basic recipe, replacing half the raisins with 1/2 cup chopped fresh or canned peaches.

whole wheat fruit & zucchini bran muffins
Prepare the basic recipe, replacing half the raisins with 1/2 cup of cooked and chopped zucchini.

whole wheat trail mix muffins
Prepare the basic recipe, replacing the rolled oats with a store-bought trail mix.

variations

banana, cranberry & walnut muffins

see base recipe page 134

banana, peach & almond muffins
Prepare the basic recipe, replacing the vanilla extract with almond extract, the walnuts with almonds, and the cranberries with 1/2 cup chopped canned or fresh peaches.

banana, apple & cinnamon muffins
Prepare the basic recipe, replacing the cranberries with 1/2 cup peeled, cored, and chopped apples. Add 2 teaspoons ground cinnamon to the dry ingredients.

banana, mocha & pecan muffins
Prepare the basic recipe, replacing the cranberries and walnuts with 1/2 cup semisweet chocolate chips and 3/4 cup chopped pecans. Add 3 teaspoons instant coffee granules to the dry ingredients.

whole wheat banana, cranberry & walnut muffins
Prepare the basic recipe, replacing 1 cup of the all-purpose flour with 1 cup whole wheat flour.

variations

heart-friendly muffins

see base recipe page 137

heart-friendly fig & bran muffins
Prepare the basic recipe, replacing half the blueberries with 1 cup chopped
dried figs and replacing 1/4 cup all-purpose flour with 1/4 cup wheat bran.

heart-friendly date & walnut muffins
Prepare the basic recipe, omitting 1/2 cup blueberries and adding 1/4 cup
chopped dates, 1/4 cup raisins, and 1/2 cup chopped walnuts.

heart-friendly golden raisin & bran muffins
Prepare the basic recipe, replacing 1/2 cup blueberries with 1/2 cup golden
raisins and 1/4 cup all-purpose flour with 1/4 cup wheat bran.

heart-friendly spicy apple & oatmeal muffins
Prepare the basic recipe, replacing the blueberries with 3/4 cup peeled, cored,
and chopped apples and 1/2 cup of the all-purpose flour with 1/2 cup rolled
oats. Add 2 teaspoons pumpkin pie spice to the dry ingredients.

heart-friendly muffins with ginger
Prepare the basic recipe, adding 1/4 cup chopped crystallized ginger to the
dry ingredients.

variations

parmesan & pine nut muffins

see base recipe page 138

tuna & olive muffins
Prepare the basic recipe, omitting the cheese, pine nuts, and mustard.
Substitute 1/4 cup pitted, chopped black olives and 1 (6-ounce) can of
tuna in oil, drained and flaked. Omit the topping.

chicken & corn muffins
Prepare the basic recipe, omitting the Parmesan, pine nuts, and mustard.
Substitute 1/3 cup canned whole kernel corn and 1/2 cup chopped cooked
chicken breast. Replace the topping with a sprinkling of paprika.

spicy sausage & onion muffins
Prepare the basic recipe, replacing the Parmesan and pine nuts with 1/4 cup
cooked and chopped spicy sausage and 1/4 cup cooked chopped onion. Omit
the topping.

spinach, parmesan & pine nut muffins
Prepare the basic recipe, adding 1/3 cup cooked, chopped, and drained spinach.

crispy bacon & cheese muffins
Prepare the basic recipe, replacing the Parmesan and pine nuts with 1/3 cup
shredded cheddar Cheese and 1/4 cup crisply cooked and crumbled bacon.

variations

flaky croissants

see base recipe page 140

chocolate-filled croissants
Prepare the basic recipe, but just before rolling up the dough, place a small square of chocolate at the wide edge of the triangle.

almond croissants
Prepare the basic recipe, but just before rolling up the dough, place a small ball of almond paste at the wide edge of the triangle. Scatter a few sliced almonds over the tops of all the croissants before baking.

croissants with raisins
Prepare the basic recipe, but just before rolling up the dough, sprinkle a teaspoon of raisins over the dough and press them in slightly.

ham & cheese breakfast croissant sandwich
Prepare the basic recipe. Slice croissants in half, add 2 slices of ham and 1 slice American cheese per croissant, and warm in oven to melt the cheese.

snack-size croissants
Prepare the basic recipe. Instead of dividing the dough into 4 parts, divide into 8 parts. Roll into circles 6 inches across, then follow the basic recipe.

eggs

Eggs are pure protein and very versatile. Low in calories and carbohydrates, they are the ideal food to sustain you until lunchtime. They are quick and easy to cook, go with anything, and you'll never get tired of them.

perfect poached eggs

see variations page 172

If you know how to make poached eggs perfectly, then you can make lots of perfect egg dishes for any number of people. Make sure you have everything on hand before you start to cook, as these eggs take very little time to prepare.

2 eggs
1 tsp. white vinegar
hot buttered toast, to serve

Crack the eggs into small ramekins and set aside. Fill a medium saucepan two-thirds full with water, add white vinegar, and bring to a boil. Turn the heat down and get the water to a rolling boil, that is, just past the simmering point, but not so that the bubbles are moving really strongly. If the water is boiling too much, it will disperse the egg as you tip it in.

When you are happy with the water, take a dinner knife and swirl the water around to create a vortex in the middle, and tip your egg into the middle. The water swirling around the edge will help keep the egg together. Time the egg for 2 1/2 minutes (for a large egg). It will start to rise to the surface as it cooks. Lift out carefully with a slotted spoon and drain on paper towel. Repeat with the other egg. Serve on hot buttered toast.

Serves 2

soft-boiled eggs & soldiers

see variations page 173

You've been told never to play with your food, but break the rules for once and enjoy dipping toast "soldiers" into runny egg yolk. Always buy the same size eggs and you will get to know the exact timing for how thick or runny you like your soft-boiled egg to be.

2 eggs
2-4 slices thick white bread
butter, for spreading

Place your eggs in a saucepan of cold water and put pan on a burner. Turn the heat to the highest setting and bring to a boil, uncovered. As soon as the water starts to boil, lower the heat and simmer for between 3 and 5 minutes, depending on the size of the egg. Practice and experience are important.

Meanwhile, toast the bread slices on both sides under the broiler or in a toaster, spread them with butter, and cut them into strips.

Remove the eggs from the pan with a slotted spoon, place in egg cups, and surround with the toast strips. Serve immediately.

Serves 2

ham & cheese soufflé

see variations page 174

Soufflés need to be served as soon as they come out of the oven, as they can deflate quite quickly.

1/3 cup butter, plus extra for greasing
1/2 cup flour
2/3 cup whole milk
3 large eggs, separated
2/3 cup finely chopped ham

1 tsp. Dijon-style mustard
1 cup shredded Cheddar cheese, plus 1 tbsp.
   for sprinkling
salt and freshly ground black pepper

Heat the oven to 375°F and liberally butter a 1-quart soufflé dish. Melt butter in a large saucepan, add the flour, and cook for a minute, stirring constantly. Remove from the heat and gradually stir in the milk. Return to the heat and bring to a boil, stirring all the time, until it becomes a thick sauce that leaves the sides of the pan.

Stir in the egg yolks, ham, mustard, and 1 cup cheese. Season with salt and freshly ground black pepper. Keep over the heat, stirring all the time, until the cheese has melted. Remove from the heat.

In a clean, streak-free bowl, whisk the egg whites until stiff peaks form. Fold whites into the cheese sauce with a metal spoon. Turn mixture into the buttered soufflé dish and run a teaspoon around the outside edge of the mixture, pushing it inward to prevent the soufflé spilling over when cooking. Sprinkle 1 tablespoon shredded Cheddar over the top, and bake for 40 minutes until well risen and golden brown. Remove from oven and serve immediately.

Serves 4

breakfast frittata

see variations page 175

A frittata (an Italian word for an omelet) is baked in the oven. This one combines some of the best elements of traditional breakfast fare.

1 tbsp. olive oil, plus extra for greasing
8 large eggs
1/4 cup sour cream
salt and freshly ground black pepper
5 strips bacon, chopped into bite-size pieces

1 cup sliced button mushrooms
5 cooked sausage links, cut into bite-size pieces
4 cooked, peeled potatoes, cut into bite-size pieces
1 tbsp. freshly chopped parsley

Heat the oven to 350°F and grease a 9x13-inch rectangular baking dish with olive oil. In a large bowl, whisk the eggs, then whisk in the sour cream and salt and pepper to taste. Set aside.

In a large skillet, heat 1 tablespoon oil, and fry the bacon and mushrooms until nicely browned and slightly caramelized. Add the sausage links, potato pieces, and parsley, and heat through.

Tip the contents of the pan into the baking dish, then pour in the egg mixture. Bake for about 35 minutes, or until the egg has risen and set. Serve immediately.

Serves 4

ultimate spanish tortilla

see variations page 176

A Spanish tortilla is a thick omelet made with potatoes and onions.

6 or 7 potatoes, peeled
4 tbsp. olive oil
1 small onion, finely chopped
salt and freshly ground black pepper
8 large eggs

In a large saucepan, boil the potatoes for 10 minutes. Drain, let cool, then thinly slice. In a skillet, heat the oil, then fry the onion until softened. Add the sliced potatoes and fry until lightly browned, not crisp. Season with salt and freshly ground black pepper.

In a bowl, whisk the eggs, then pour them into the skillet on top of the potatoes and onions. Cook over medium heat until the eggs have just set and the bottom has browned. Turn the tortilla out onto a plate, then slide it back into the pan to cook the other side. (Alternatively, after cooking the first side, heat the broiler and grill the top of the tortilla until browned.) Serve immediately, cut into wedges.

Serves 4

mexican scrambled eggs

see variations page 177

Scrambled eggs are a good foundation for a multitude of flavorful ingredients. This Mexican recipe, with its fried tortilla strips, tomatoes, and jalapeño pepper, can be easily varied.

3 tbsp. vegetable oil
3 soft corn tortillas
2 fresh tomatoes, seeded and chopped
3 scallions, chopped

1 green jalapeño pepper, seeded and chopped
8 eggs, beaten
salt and freshly ground black pepper
2 tbsp. freshly chopped cilantro, to garnish

In a large skillet, heat the vegetable oil. Roll up the tortillas and slice them into strips directly into the hot oil. Fry them for a few minutes until crisp, then remove them from the pan and drain on a paper towel.

Add the chopped tomatoes, scallions, and jalapeño to the skillet, and fry together for 2 minutes. Tip the tortillas back into the pan and add the beaten eggs. Season to taste with salt and pepper. Stir with a wooden spoon to scramble the eggs. Once the eggs start to set, remove the skillet from the heat and continue to stir until cooked to your liking. Serve immediately, sprinkled with chopped cilantro.

Serves 4

crabmeat strata

see variations page 178

This is a very rich and creamy dish, especially good for a holiday brunch buffet. It can be prepared up to 24 hours in advance.

butter, for greasing
6 thick slices white bread, cut into cubes
2 (6-oz.) cans crabmeat or 1 lb. fresh crabmeat, picked over
1 cup shredded Gruyère cheese
1 cup shredded Cheddar cheese

4 scallions, roughly chopped
6 large eggs, lightly beaten
1 1/3 cups milk
2 tbsp. dry sherry or apple juice
1 tbsp. Dijon-style mustard
1 tbsp. Worcestershire sauce

Grease a 2-quart casserole dish with butter. In a large bowl, mix together the bread, crabmeat, cheeses, and scallions. Add the remaining ingredients and stir well to combine. Pour into the casserole, cover, and chill for 2 to 24 hours.

Heat the oven to 350°F. Remove the cover from the casserole and bake for about 45 minutes, or until a knife inserted in the middle comes out clean. Let it stand for 10 minutes before serving.

Serves 6-8

squash, sage & gruyère frittata

see variations page 179

These are some interesting flavors for breakfast, if you fancy something a little different.

2 tbsp. butter
2 1/2 cups summer squash in 1/4-inch cubes
   (about 2 medium squash)
2 tbsp. freshly chopped sage

8 large eggs
1/4 cup water
3/4 cup shredded Gruyère cheese
salt and freshly ground black pepper

In a large ovenproof skillet, melt the butter, add the squash, and sauté for about 8-10 minutes. Stir in the sage. Cook until the squash is tender and slightly browned.

Heat the broiler. In a large bowl, whisk the eggs and water together, and stir in half the cheese. Season with salt and pepper and pour over the squash in the skillet. Reduce the heat, cover, and cook for a few minutes until the eggs are beginning to set on the bottom but the top is still a little loose. Remove the cover, sprinkle the remaining cheese on top, and place skillet under the broiler. Broil just until set and the cheese is melted. Let stand for 10 minutes, then serve, cut into wedges.

Serves 4-5

eggs florentine

see variations page 180

Once you've perfected your poached egg technique, there are many ways to turn them into a delicious, filling breakfast, such as this one with spinach, hollandaise sauce, and English muffins.

2 egg yolks
2 tbsp. hot water
2/3 cup butter, melted
juice of 1/2 lemon
salt and freshly ground black pepper
pinch cayenne pepper

1/4 cup butter for cooking and spreading
3 cups fresh spinach leaves
4 poached eggs (page 155)
2 English muffins, split

First make a hollandaise sauce. Place the egg yolks in a heat-resistant glass bowl over a pan of simmering water and whisk with 2 tablespoons hot water. Very slowly, add the melted butter. Do not add the milky residue at the bottom of the melted butter. Whisk until all the butter has been incorporated. Whisk in the lemon juice, and season with salt and a pinch of cayenne pepper. Set aside.

In a large skillet, melt a little butter and add the spinach. Stir until wilted, then drain and season with salt and pepper. Remove from heat. Heat the broiler, and broil the muffins until lightly browned. Spread with butter and divide the spinach between them, leaving a slight indentation on top in which to place the poached eggs, one on each muffin half. Spoon a quarter of the hollandaise over each egg, then place them underneath the broiler for 1 minute. Serve immediately.

Serves 2-4

bacon & egg tarts

see variations page 181

Make these tarts when you want to impress your guests.

1 tbsp. butter for greasing
10 oz. short-crust pastry (homemade or
   store-bought)
8 strips bacon, chopped
1 small onion, finely chopped

2 large eggs
2/3 cup half-and-half
salt and freshly ground black pepper
2 tbsp. freshly chopped parsley

Preheat the oven to 400°F, and grease 4 individual 4-inch tart pans with butter.

On a lightly floured surface, roll out the pastry, then grease and line the 4 tart pans. Line
pastry with waxed paper, fill with baking beans, and bake for 10 minutes. Remove the paper
and beans and bake for 5 more minutes. Remove pans from the oven.

In a skillet, fry the bacon for a few minutes, add the onion, and continue to cook until the
onion has softened and the bacon is crisp. Divide the bacon and onion between the tart
pans. In a bowl, whisk the eggs and half-and-half together, and season with salt and pepper.
Stir in the parsley. Divide mixture between the tart pans.

Place the tart pans on a cookie sheet (which makes it easier to move them in and out of the
oven). Bake for about 15-20 minutes, until the eggs have set and the tarts are golden brown.
Serve immediately.

Serves 4

variations

perfect poached eggs

see base recipe page 155

poached eggs on crushed potatoes

Prepare the basic recipe, but instead of serving the eggs on hot buttered toast, serve on boiled potatoes, crushed with a little butter and parsley.

poached eggs with asparagus

Prepare the basic recipe, but instead of serving the eggs on hot buttered toast, serve with some steamed asparagus, dressed with melted butter and parsley.

poached eggs with bagels

Prepare the basic recipe, but instead of serving the eggs on hot buttered toast, serve them on halved bagels, spread with a little cream cheese or butter.

poached eggs with mushrooms & ham

Prepare the basic recipe, but instead of serving the eggs on hot buttered toast, serve them on portobello mushrooms.

soft-boiled eggs & soldiers

see base recipe page 156

hard-boiled eggs with bagel soldiers

Prepare the basic recipe, boiling the eggs for an extra 7 or 8 minutes. Remove from heat and put the eggs into iced water for 5 minutes. Remove shells, mash eggs with a little mayonnaise, add salt and pepper to taste, and spread on bagels cut into soldiers.

soft-boiled eggs with sausage dippers

Prepare the basic recipe, replacing the bread and butter with cooked sausage links to dip in the egg.

soft-boiled eggs with asparagus

Prepare the basic recipe, replacing the bread and butter with steamed asparagus to dip in the egg.

soft-boiled eggs with thick oven fries

Prepare the basic recipe, replacing the bread and butter with thick oven fries. Peel and slice a large potato into thick strips, coat with vegetable oil, and bake at 400°F for 30 minutes. Serve hot with the eggs.

variations

ham & cheese soufflé

see base recipe page 159

mushroom & cheese soufflé
Prepare the basic recipe, replacing the ham with 1 cup cooked, sliced button mushrooms.

ham, cheese & onion soufflé
Prepare the basic recipe, adding 1 finely chopped onion. Sauté for a few minutes in the melted butter before adding the flour.

ham & double cheese soufflé
Prepare the basic recipe, replacing half the Cheddar cheese with Monterey Jack cheese.

ham, cheese & spinach soufflé
Prepare the basic recipe, adding 2/3 cup cooked, well-drained, chopped spinach to the mixture.

tuna & cheese soufflé
Prepare the basic recipe, replacing the ham with canned tuna, drained and flaked.

variations

breakfast frittata

see base recipe page 160

potato, apple & tuna frittata
Prepare the basic recipe, omitting the bacon and sausage and adding 1 peeled, cored, and chopped apple and 1 can (6-ounce) tuna, drained and flaked, before mixing with the eggs.

smoked salmon frittata
Prepare the basic recipe, omitting the bacon and sausage. Add 1 cup chopped smoked salmon before mixing with the eggs.

cheese & onion frittata
Prepare the basic recipe, omitting the sausage. Add 1 finely chopped onion and cook it with the bacon. Stir 1 cup shredded Cheddar cheese into the eggs.

feta & pepper frittata
Prepare the basic recipe, omitting the bacon and sausage, and adding 1 seeded and sliced red bell pepper to the mixture with the mushrooms, and 1/2 cup chopped feta with the parsley.

variations

ultimate spanish tortilla

see base recipe page 162

spanish tortilla with cheese & leeks
Prepare the basic recipe, adding 1 chopped leek to the skillet with the onion, and 2/3 cup shredded Cheddar cheese to the skillet with the eggs.

spanish tortilla with parma ham & basil
Prepare the basic recipe, adding 1/2 cup chopped Parma ham and 3 tablespoons freshly shredded basil to the skillet with the eggs.

spanish tortilla with chorizo & parsley
Prepare the basic recipe, adding 1/2 cup chopped chorizo and 3 tablespoons freshly chopped parsley to the skillet with the eggs.

spanish tortilla with green onion & peas
Prepare the basic recipe, adding 3 chopped green onions and 1/3 cup frozen peas to the skillet with the eggs.

variations

mexican scrambled eggs

see base recipe page 163

mexican scrambled eggs with vegetables
Prepare the basic recipe, adding 1/4 cup each of finely chopped red bell pepper, mushrooms, and Spanish onion to the skillet with the tomatoes.

spanish scrambled eggs
Prepare the basic recipe, omitting the jalapeño pepper and substituting 1/4 cup spicy chorizo sausage, chopped into tiny cubes.

french scrambled eggs
Prepare the basic recipe, omitting the tortilla, jalapeño pepper, and cilantro. Substitute 1/4 cup cooked potato, cut into tiny cubes, 1 crushed garlic clove, and parsley.

swiss scrambled eggs
Prepare the basic recipe, omitting the jalapeño pepper and substituting cooked and finely shredded potato to the eggs.

variations

crabmeat strata

see base recipe page 164

smoked salmon strata
Prepare the basic recipe, replacing the crabmeat with canned red salmon, drained and flaked.

shrimp, egg & parsley strata
Prepare the basic recipe, replacing the crabmeat with 1/2 cup cooked small shrimp, 2 chopped hard-boiled eggs and 2 tablespoons freshly chopped parsley.

crab & tuna strata
Prepare the basic recipe, replacing 1 can crabmeat with 1 can tuna, drained and flaked.

mushroom, leek & cheese strata
Prepare the basic recipe, omitting the crabmeat and substituting 1 cup cooked and sliced mushrooms and 1/2 cup cooked and chopped leeks.

smoked mackerel & tomato strata
Prepare the basic recipe, replacing the crabmeat with smoked mackerel, bones removed, and chopped. Add 2 tomatoes, seeded and chopped.

variations

squash, sage & gruyère frittata

see base recipe page 166

zucchini, thyme & gruyère frittata
Prepare the basic recipe, replacing the summer squash with zucchini and the sage with fresh thyme leaves.

carrot, cilantro & gruyère frittata
Prepare the basic recipe, replacing the squash with 2 1/2 cups boiled and chopped carrots and the sage with fresh cilantro.

broccoli, oregano & gruyère frittata
Prepare the basic recipe, replacing the squash with 2 1/2 cups cooked and chopped broccoli and the sage with fresh oregano.

squash, scallion, pancetta & gruyère frittata
Prepare the basic recipe, adding 4 chopped scallions and 1/2 cup chopped pancetta to the skillet with the sage.

variations

eggs florentine

see base recipe page 169

eggs benedict
Prepare the basic recipe, replacing the spinach with a slice of Canadian bacon or ham, lightly sautéed in a little butter, on each muffin.

sausage & tomato eggs benedict
Prepare the basic recipe, replacing the spinach with a cooked sausage patty (homemade if desired; see recipe page 233) topped with a slice of tomato, sautéed lightly in butter.

eggs florentine with cheese
Prepare the basic recipe, adding a slice of cheese on top of the muffin before you add the poached egg.

eggs florentine with mustard hollandaise
Prepare the basic recipe, adding 1 teaspoon Dijon mustard to the hollandaise.

bacon & egg tarts

see base recipe page 170

roasted red bell pepper & chorizo tarts
Prepare the basic recipe, replacing the bacon with 1 seeded and chopped
roasted red bell pepper and 1/2 cup chopped chorizo sausage.

sausage & tomato tarts
Prepare the basic recipe, replacing the bacon with 1/2 cup chopped sausages
and 2 seeded and chopped fresh tomatoes.

bacon, swiss cheese & onion tarts
Prepare the basic recipe, adding 1/2 cup shredded Gruyère cheese to the
tart pans.

mediterranean tarts
Prepare the basic recipe, adding 1/4 cup chopped sun-dried tomatoes and
1/4 cup pitted and chopped black olives to the tart pans.

crabmeat tarts
Prepare the basic recipe, omitting the bacon and substituting 1/2 cup
canned crabmeat, drained. Add 2 teaspoons freshly chopped cilantro.

pancakes, waffles & french toast

This is one of my favorite chapters. Pancakes,

waffles and French toast recipes are what I turn to

when giving my grandchildren (and myself!) a

special breakfast treat.

apple pancakes with maple syrup butter

see variations page 201

These are sometimes called German apple pancakes.

1/2 cup (1 stick) butter, softened
1/4 cup maple syrup
1 1/2 cups flour
2 tbsp. rolled oats
2 tbsp. wheat bran
1/2 tsp. baking soda
2 tsp. baking powder
2 tsp. sugar

1/4 tsp. salt
2 large eggs
1 1/2 cups buttermilk
1/4 cup whole milk
4 tbsp. butter, plus 1 tbsp. for cooking
1 Granny Smith apple, peeled, cored,
    thinly sliced
powdered sugar, to serve

First make the maple butter. Beat the 1/2 cup butter and maple syrup together with an electric mixer until blended. Set aside. In a large bowl, mix all the dry ingredients together. In another bowl, whisk together the eggs, buttermilk, and milk. Make a well in the center of the flour mixture, and pour in the egg mixture. Stir with a wooden spoon from the center, slowly incorporating the flour from the sides as you stir. Do not overmix or worry about small lumps. In a large skillet, melt the 4 tablespoons butter, then tip it into the batter. Put the skillet back on the heat, add the 1 tablespoon butter, swirl it around the pan, and when it is good and hot, add large spoonfuls of batter to make 5-inch pancakes. Place a few apple slices on top of each pancake and press down into the batter. Cook for about 3 minutes, or until golden, and turn. Cook another 2 minutes. Serve immediately with the apple on top, a dusting of powdered sugar, and maple butter on the side.

Makes 10 pancakes

classic blueberry pancakes

see variations page 202

How about starting your day with a fluffy blueberry pancake, spread with butter, sprinkled with powdered sugar, and drizzled with delicious maple syrup?

3 cups fresh blueberries
1 3/4 cups flour
3 tsp. baking powder
2 tsp. sugar
good pinch of salt
2 medium eggs

1 cup milk
1 tsp. vanilla extract
4 tablespoons butter, for the batter
    and cooking
powdered sugar, maple syrup, and butter,
    to serve

Heat the oven to 275°F. Divide the blueberries into 8 portions. Sift the dry ingredients into a large bowl. Make a well in the center, break in the eggs, and add the milk and vanilla. Stir from the center with a wooden spoon, slowly incorporating the flour from the sides as you stir. Do not overmix and do not worry about any lumps. In a large skillet, melt 2 tablespoons butter, and then tip it into the batter, and stir it in lightly. Put the skillet back on the heat, add a little more butter, and swirl it around the base of the pan. When it is nice and hot, but not smoking, spoon about 3 tablespoons of batter into the pan to form a pancake about 5 inches in diameter. Spoon in 3 tablespoons more, forming another pancake. Drop a portion of blueberries on top of the pancakes, and press them slightly into the batter. The pancakes should make a sizzling sound and begin to bubble at once. When they look dry at the edges, turn them over. They should have a good brown color. The second side will cook faster than the first. Place them on a platter, cover, and keep in the warm oven while you make the rest. Serve dusted with powdered sugar, with butter and maple syrup on the side.

Makes 8 pancakes

bacon & parsley hotcakes

see variations page 203

Not everyone likes sweet pancakes in the morning. Not only are these pancakes savory and not sweet, they also have protein in them, which is good for keeping you energized until lunch. They're delicious served with oven-roasted vine tomatoes (see page 254).

8 strips bacon, finely chopped
3/4 cup flour
1/2 cup finely grated Cheddar cheese
1 tsp. chopped fresh thyme leaves
2 tbsp. chopped fresh parsley

salt and freshly ground black pepper to taste
2 eggs
6 tbsp. milk
2 tbsp. sunflower oil for frying (or canola oil)

Fry the bacon until crisp and golden, then drain on paper towels. In a bowl, mix the flour, cheese, herbs, bacon, salt, and pepper. Make a well in the center, break in the eggs, and add the milk. Stir with a wooden spoon from the center, slowly incorporating the flour from the sides as you stir. Do not overmix. You should have a fairly thick batter.

In a large skillet, heat a little sunflower oil. When it is hot, drop in large spoonfuls of the batter. Cook until the hotcakes start to look dry at the edges, then turn them, and cook the other side until golden brown. Keep warm while you make the rest. Serve right away.

Makes 8 pancakes

chunky monkey pancakes

see variations page 204

Children love the name of these pancakes, and with bananas, chocolate, and pecans they love the taste, too.

1 3/4 cups all-purpose flour
3 tsp. baking powder
2 tsp. sugar
1/4 cup chopped pecans
good pinch salt
2 small eggs

1 cup milk
2 tbsp. butter, plus extra for cooking
2 bananas, sliced
1 cup semisweet chocolate chips
powdered sugar, maple syrup, and whipped
    cream to serve

Preheat the oven to 275°F. In a large bowl, mix the flour, baking powder, sugar, pecans, and salt. Make a well in the center, break in the eggs, and add the milk. Stir with a wooden spoon from the center, slowly incorporating the flour from the sides as you stir. Do not overmix.

Melt 2 tablespoons butter in a large skillet, then tip it into the batter. Add a little more butter to the pan, and when the pan is hot, drop in large spoonfuls of batter to make 5-inch pancakes. Drop a few slices of banana and some chocolate chips onto each pancake, pressing them into the batter slightly. They should make a sizzling sound and begin to bubble at once. When they look dry at the edges, turn them over. They should have a good brown color. The second side will cook faster than the first. Place pancakes on a platter and keep warm in oven while you make the rest. Serve with a dusting of powdered sugar, maple syrup, and whipped cream.

Makes 10 pancakes

stuffed savory ham & cheese french toast

see variations page 205

Butter burns easily when heated—add a little vegetable oil and it will not burn so readily.

4 oz. cream cheese, softened
1 cup shredded Cheddar cheese
2 scallions, finely chopped
salt and freshly ground black pepper to taste
4 slices ham (black forest preferably)
8 thick slices day-old white bread

4 eggs
1/2 cup milk
few shakes of hot sauce, to taste
butter and vegetable oil, for cooking
powdered sugar and maple syrup, to serve

In a medium bowl, mix the cream cheese and Cheddar with the scallions. Season with salt and pepper. Spread 4 slices of bread generously with the filling, lay a slice of ham on top of each one, and top with the remaining bread slices, making 4 sandwiches.

In a shallow dish, whisk together the eggs, milk, salt, pepper, and hot sauce. Dip each sandwich in the batter, turning to coat both sides, and allowing each side to soak up some of the batter. Do not soak too long or the sandwiches will fall apart when you lift them.

In a large skillet, heat a little butter and vegetable oil. When it is good and hot, lay some sandwiches in the skillet, and cook them to a rich brown. Turn and cook the other side. Keep warm while you make the rest. Serve immediately, with a sprinkling of powdered sugar and with maple syrup on the side.

Serves 4

almond waffles with apricot sauce

see variations page 206

Almonds and apricots are a classic combination, and the buttermilk gives a lovely tangy richness to this waffle.

for the apricot sauce
1 (16-oz.) can apricots
1 1/2 cups brown sugar

for the waffles
1 1/2 cups flour
1 tsp. baking soda
2 tsp. baking powder

1/2 tsp. salt
2 tbsp. sugar
1/2 cup finely chopped almonds
1 2/3 cups buttermilk
1 tsp. almond extract
2 tbsp. butter, melted, plus more for cooking
3 eggs, separated
powdered sugar, to serve

First make the apricot sauce. Strain the apricots, reserving the juice. Chop the apricots. Place the apricots, juice, and brown sugar in a medium saucepan over medium heat. Bring to a boil and simmer for 5-6 minutes. Preheat the waffle iron. In a large bowl, sift together the flour, baking soda, baking powder, salt, and sugar. Stir in the almonds. In another bowl, beat together the buttermilk, almond extract, 2 tablespoons cooled melted butter, and egg yolks. Stir the flour mixture into the milk mixture, and beat well to make a smooth batter. In a clean bowl, whisk the egg whites until stiff peaks form, then gently fold them into the batter with a metal spoon. Do not overmix. Once your waffle iron is hot, brush with a little butter, and spoon in enough batter to just cover the base. Remember the batter will rise and spread during cooking. Cook until crisp and golden, about 3-4 minutes. Keep warm while you make the rest, then serve immediately, sprinkled with a little powdered sugar, with the apricot sauce on the side.

Makes 8 large waffles

cheddar & mushroom crêpes

see variations page 207

The crêpe is a wonderfully versatile pancake to serve at any time of day, and you can fill it with so many different ingredients. This is a favorite recipe.

1 tbsp. canola oil
2 cups sliced button mushrooms
1/2 cup shredded Cheddar cheese,
  plus extra to garnish

for the batter
1 cup all-purpose flour
pinch salt
1 large egg, lightly beaten
1 1/4 cups milk
oil, for brushing
chopped fresh parsley, to garnish

Heat the oven to 375°F and grease the base and sides of a casserole dish. In a medium saucepan, heat the oil and add the mushrooms. Sauté for about 7 minutes until all the liquid has come out. Drain on a paper towel, then place in a bowl. Set aside.

To make the crêpes, sift the flour and salt into a large bowl. Using a wooden spoon, make a well in the center, and break in the egg. Gradually add half the milk, stirring from the center, and slowly incorporate the flour from the sides as you stir. When all the flour is mixed in, beat the mixture with the wooden spoon or an electric mixer, until it becomes smooth and free of lumps. Allow the batter to stand for a few minutes, then add the remainder of the milk, beating continuously, until the batter is bubbly and has a smooth consistency.

Heat a nonstick skillet, and brush lightly with oil. The pan should be really hot before you add the batter. Using a pitcher or a ladle, pour in just enough batter to flow in a thin film over the base, tilting the pan to spread it. The heat is right if the underside of the crêpe

becomes golden in 1 minute. Using a palette knife, flip the crêpe over and cook the other side. Keep warm while you make the rest. Mix the cooled mushrooms with the cheese and divide between all 8 crêpes, folding the sides over to encase the filling.

Place side by side in the greased casserole dish and top with extra grated cheese. Bake for just 10 minutes to melt the cheese. Serve immediately, sprinkled with parsley.

Serves 4

chocolate chip waffles

see variations page 208

The smell of these cooking will get everyone out of bed in double-quick time.

for the chocolate sauce
1 1/4 cups heavy cream
8 oz. bittersweet chocolate, broken into pieces
1 tbsp. light corn syrup

for the waffles
1 1/2 cups flour
1 1/2 tsp. baking powder

2 tbsp. sugar
1/2 cup semisweet chocolate chips
1/2 tsp. salt
1 1/4 cups milk
2 large eggs
5 tbsp. butter, melted, plus extra for cooking
powdered sugar, to serve

To make the chocolate sauce, heat the cream in a medium saucepan until almost boiling. Add the chocolate and corn syrup, and stir until the chocolate has melted and the sauce is smooth and creamy. Serve hot or cold.

Preheat the waffle iron. In a large bowl, using a fork, mix together the flour, baking powder, sugar, chocolate chips, and salt. In another bowl, whisk the milk and eggs together, then pour into the flour mixture. Mix together with the fork until there are no large lumps, but do not overmix. Stir in the 5 tablespoons melted butter. When the iron is hot, lightly brush it with some melted butter, then spoon in enough batter to just cover the base. Remember the batter will rise and spread during cooking. Cook for 3-5 minutes, until crisp. Keep warm while you make the rest. Serve immediately, sprinkled with a little powdered sugar and with the chocolate sauce on the side.

Makes 8 waffles

bacon waffles with sausage gravy

see variations page 209

Sausage gravy is usually served over biscuits, but it also works well with waffles.

for the bacon
10 strips bacon
1/4 cup brown sugar

for the sausage gravy
1 lb. pork sausage, crumbled
2 tbsp. finely chopped onion
1 tbsp. vegetable oil
5 tbsp. flour
3 cups milk
1 or 2 chicken stock cubes, crumbled

salt and freshly ground black pepper to taste
1/2 tsp. freshly chopped sage

for the waffles
1 1/2 cups flour
1 1/2 tsp. baking powder
2 tbsp. sugar
1/2 tsp. salt
2 large eggs
1 1/4 cups milk
5 tbsp. melted butter, plus extra for cooking

Prepare the bacon. Preheat the oven to 375°F and line a cookie sheet with foil. Grease the foil with a little vegetable oil and arrange the bacon strips side by side in a single layer on top. Sprinkle generously with brown sugar and bake in the top of the oven until the bacon is crisp and the sugar is caramelized, about 10-15 minutes. Remove from the oven and, with tongs, place the bacon on a cutting board (not on paper towels). When cool, chop very small. To make sausage gravy, in a large skillet, fry sausage and onion in a little oil until brown and cooked through. Drain off all but 2-3 tablespoons drippings. Stir the flour into the sausage and drippings until blended. Cook for 2 or 3 minutes, and gradually add the milk, stirring continually, until it starts to simmer and becomes a thick sauce. Crumble in the stock cubes, and season with salt and pepper. Cover and keep warm.

Preheat waffle iron. Mix all the dry ingredients in a large bowl. In another bowl, whisk the eggs and milk, then pour into the dry ingredients. Using a fork, fold together very lightly until there are no large lumps. Stir in the bacon bits. Do not overmix. Pour in 5 tablespoons melted butter, and give one last stir.

When the waffle iron is hot, lightly brush it with a little butter and spoon in enough batter to just cover the base. Remember the batter will spread and rise during cooking. Cook for 3-5 minutes until waffle is crisp and golden. Keep warm while you make the rest. Serve immediately with sausage gravy on the side.

Makes 10 waffles

apple & pecan french toast

see variations page 210

This is a great way to use up leftover panettone or brioche, but any type of day-old white bread will be good (day-old bread is always better than fresh for French toast).

4 tbsp. butter
1/4 cup sugar
2 tsp. vanilla extract
1/2 tsp. ground cinnamon
pinch salt
1/4 tsp. ground nutmeg
4 apples, peeled, cored, and chopped
4 large eggs
3 tbsp. molasses

1/2 cup heavy cream
1/2 tsp. ground cinnamon
1/2 tsp. ground ginger
pinch salt
12 slices day-old white bread (or panettone, challah, or brioche)
butter and a little vegetable oil, for cooking
1 cup chopped pecans
sprinkling of powdered sugar, to serve

In a large saucepan, combine the butter, sugar, 1/2 the vanilla, cinnamon, salt, and nutmeg, and heat until sizzling. Lower the heat, and add the chopped apples. Simmer gently, stirring, until the apples are very tender and the sauce thickens and browns, about 15 minutes. Add a little water if the mixture begins to burn. Set aside to cool slightly. In a shallow dish, whisk the eggs, molasses, cream, remaining vanilla, cinnamon, ginger, and salt. Dip each slice of bread into the mixture, coating both sides, and arrange the slices in a pyramid on a plate. Melt a little butter and vegetable oil in a large skillet. When it is hot but not smoking, put in the bread slices and sprinkle a few chopped pecans on top. Press pecans lightly into the bread, and cook to a rich brown. Turn the toast and cook the other side, shaking the skillet slightly to make sure it does not stick. Remove and keep warm while you make the rest. Serve immediately with a sprinkling of powdered sugar and caramelized apples on the side.

Serves 4

overnight caramel pecan french toast

see variations page 211

Start this the night before, and it will be ready to bake in the morning. It's easy, but never fails to impress!

1 cup brown sugar
1/2 cup butter
2 tbsp. light corn syrup
1 cup chopped pecans
18 (1/2-inch-thick) slices day-old French bread
6 eggs, beaten

1 1/2 cups milk
1 tsp. vanilla extract
1 tbsp. sugar
1 1/2 tsp. ground cinnamon
1/2 tsp. ground nutmeg

For the caramel, mix together the brown sugar, butter, and corn syrup in a medium saucepan. Heat and stir until the butter is melted and the brown sugar dissolved. Pour into an ungreased 9x13-inch rectangular baking dish and sprinkle with half the pecans.

Arrange half of the bread slices in a single layer on top of the caramel, sprinkle with the rest of the pecans, and top with the remaining bread slices. In a medium bowl, whisk together the eggs, milk, and vanilla, and carefully pour over the bread. Press lightly with the back of a spoon to moisten the bread. In a small bowl, mix together the sugar, cinnamon, and nutmeg, and sprinkle over the bread. Cover and chill for 8-24 hours.

Preheat the oven to 350°F. Remove the cover, and bake for 30–40 minutes, until lightly browned. Let stand for 10 minutes. To serve, remove individual portions with a spatula and invert onto serving plates. Dust with powdered sugar and provide maple syrup on the side.

Serves 9

variations

apple pancakes with maple syrup butter

see base recipe page 183

apple & walnut pancakes with maple syrup butter
Prepare the basic recipe, adding 1/3 cup chopped walnuts to the dry ingredients.

pear pancakes with maple syrup butter
Prepare the basic recipe, replacing the apple with slices of pear.

apple & cinnamon pancakes with maple syrup butter
Prepare the basic recipe, adding 2 teaspoons cinnamon to the dry ingredients.

apricot pancakes with maple syrup butter
Prepare the basic recipe, replacing the apple with slices of apricot.

apple & raisin pancakes with maple syrup butter
Prepare the basic recipe, adding 1/2 cup raisins to the dry ingredients.

variations

classic blueberry pancakes

see base recipe page 184

classic raspberry & almond pancakes
Prepare the basic recipe, replacing the blueberries with raspberries and the vanilla extract with almond extract.

classic strawberry & white chocolate pancakes
Prepare the basic recipe, replacing the blueberries with hulled and chopped strawberries and 1/2 cup white chocolate chips.

classic peaches & cream pancakes
Prepare the basic recipe, replacing the blueberries with chopped fresh or canned peaches. Serve the pancakes with a swirl of whipped cream.

classic cherry & almond pancakes
Prepare the basic recipe, replacing the blueberries with pitted and chopped cherries and the vanilla extract with almond extract.

classic gingerbread blueberry pancakes
Prepare the basic recipe, replacing 1 tablespoon milk with 1 tablespoon molasses and adding 1 tablespoon ground ginger to the mixture.

variations

bacon & parsley hotcakes

see base recipe page 187

bacon, parsley & pine nut hotcakes
Prepare the basic recipe, adding 1/2 cup pine nuts to the dry ingredients.

bacon, parsley & poppy seed hotcakes
Prepare the basic recipe, adding 2 tablespoons poppy seeds to the dry ingredients.

bacon, parsley & oatmeal hotcakes
Prepare the basic recipe, replacing 2 tablespoons flour with 2 tablespoons rolled oats.

bacon, parsley & tomato hotcakes
Prepare the basic recipe, adding 1 tomato, seeded and chopped, to the wet ingredients.

bacon, parsley & swiss hotcakes
Prepare the basic recipe, replacing the cheese with swiss cheese.

variations

chunky monkey pancakes

see base recipe page 188

white chocolate chunky monkey pancakes with raspberries
Prepare the basic recipe, replacing the semisweet chocolate chips with white chocolate chips. Replace half the banana with fresh raspberries.

toffee chip chunky monkey pancakes
Prepare the basic recipe, replacing the semisweet chocolate chips with toffee chips. Serve with caramelized apple topping (page 198).

coconut chunky monkey pancakes with raspberry coulis
Prepare the basic recipe, adding 1/4 cup sweetened flaked coconut to the dry ingredients. Serve with a raspberry coulis, made by pressing 2 cups fresh raspberries through a sieve into a medium bowl. Add 3 tablespoons sifted powdered sugar, or to taste, and stir until smooth.

double chocolate chunky monkey pancakes with chocolate sauce
Prepare the basic recipe, replacing half the semisweet chocolate chips with white chocolate chips. Serve with chocolate sauce (page 195).

variations

stuffed savory ham & cheese french toast

see base recipe page 190

stuffed savory ham, cheese & mushroom french toast
Prepare the basic recipe, adding a few sliced cooked button mushrooms to the
filling. Replace the topping with a sprinkle of paprika, just before serving.

stuffed savory cheese, onion & and pesto french toast
Prepare the basic recipe, omitting the ham and adding a teaspoon of basil pesto to
each sandwich filling. Replace the topping with a sprinkle of freshly chopped
parsley before serving.

stuffed savory ham, mustard & swiss french toast
Prepare the basic recipe, replacing the Cheddar cheese with Gruyère cheese. Spread
a teaspoon of Dijon mustard on top of each ham slice before topping with the
bread slice. Replace the topping with a little freshly chopped cilantro before serving.

stuffed savory cheese & tomato french toast
Prepare the basic recipe, omitting the ham and adding thinly sliced plum tomatoes.
Replace the topping with a sprinkle of shredded Cheddar cheese before serving.

variations

almond waffles with apricot sauce

see base recipe page 191

georgia waffles
Prepare the basic recipe, replacing the almonds with chopped pecans and the apricots with chopped canned peaches.

lemon poppy seed waffles with raspberry sauce
Prepare the basic recipe, replacing the almonds with 1 tablespoon grated lemon peel and 1 tablespoon poppy seeds. Make a raspberry sauce by mixing 3 tablespoons sugar with 1 tablespoon cornstarch in a medium saucepan. Stir in 2/3 cup orange juice and 1 (12-oz) package frozen raspberries. Over medium heat, cook, stirring, until the mixture boils and thickens. Simmer for 1 minute, then remove and let cool slightly.

orange pecan waffles with butter pecan syrup
Prepare the basic recipe, replacing the almonds with chopped pecans and 1 tablespoon grated orange zest. For the topping, melt 2 tablespoons butter over medium heat, and add 1/3 cup chopped pecans. Cook until they are browned, stirring constantly, and stir in 3/4 cup maple-flavored syrup. When hot, remove from the heat and let cool slightly before serving.

variations

cheddar & mushroom crêpes

see base recipe page 192

edam & mushroom crêpes
Prepare the basic recipe, replacing the Cheddar cheese with edam cheese.

swiss cheese & corn crêpes
Prepare the basic recipe, omitting the oil and replacing the Cheddar cheese with Gruyère and the mushrooms with 1 cup whole kernel corn.

cheddar, stilton & squash crêpes
Prepare the basic recipe, omitting the oil and replacing the mushrooms with 1 1/2 cups chopped roasted yellow squash. Add 1/4 cup Stilton cheese, crumbled, to the filling.

cheddar & mushroom crêpes with brie & bacon
Prepare the basic recipe, adding 1/4 cup sliced brie and 6 strips crisp bacon, broken into bite-size pieces, to the filling.

cheddar & mushroom crêpes with cream cheese & chives
Prepare the basic recipe, adding 4 ounces cream cheese and 2 tablespoons freshly chopped chives to the filling.

variations

chocolate chip waffles

see base recipe page 195

chocolate chip & banana waffles with amaretto chocolate sauce
Prepare the basic waffles, adding 1 mashed ripe banana to the wet ingredients. Add 1 tablespoon amaretto to the sauce.

chocolate chip & peanut butter waffles with honey peanut butter syrup
Prepare the basic waffles, adding 1/4 cup creamy peanut butter, loosened with a little heavy cream, to the wet ingredients. For the syrup, over low heat, mix 1 cup honey and 1/2 cup creamy peanut butter, stirring until smooth and warm.

chocolate chip & strawberry waffles with strawberry sauce
Prepare the basic waffles, adding 1/4 cup chopped strawberries. For the sauce, mix 1 tablespoon cornstarch with 3 tablespoons sugar and 1/2 cup orange juice. Over medium heat, add 2 cups chopped strawberries, 2 tablespoons strawberry jam, and 1 tablespoon light corn syrup. Heat gently until boiling, stirring. Simmer for a minute or two, or until berries have broken down and sauce is thickened.

variations

bacon waffles with sausage gravy

see base recipe page 196

sun-dried tomato & basil waffles with italian sausage gravy
Prepare the basic recipe, omitting the bacon and substituting 1/2 cup chopped, sun-dried tomatoes and 1 tablespoon shredded fresh basil leaves. Prepare the sausage gravy with Italian sausage.

pine nut & poppy seed waffles with sausage gravy
Prepare the basic recipe, replacing the bacon with 1/4 cup pine nuts and 1 tablespoon poppy seeds.

bacon, cheese & chive waffles with sausage gravy
Prepare the basic recipe, adding 1/4 cup finely grated Parmesan cheese and 2 tablespoons freshly chopped chives to the dry ingredients.

turkey bacon waffles with turkey sausage gravy
Prepare the basic recipe, replacing the bacon with turkey bacon and the sausage with turkey sausage.

variations

apple & pecan french toast

see base recipe page 198

walnut french toast with caramelized apples & raisins
Prepare the basic recipe, replacing the pecans with walnuts. For the topping,
add 2 tablespoons raisins to the apples during cooking.

citrus pecan french toast with lemon topping
Prepare the basic recipe, adding the grated zest of 1 orange to the custard.
Instead of the apples, place 1 or 2 tablespoons canned lemon pie filling on
top of each portion, and add a swirl of whipped cream, if desired.

cinnamon pecan french toast with caramelized apples
Prepare the basic recipe, adding an extra 2 teaspoons ground cinnamon to
the dry ingredients.

bourbon french toast with caramelized apples & walnuts
Prepare the basic recipe, adding 2 tablespoons bourbon to the custard.
For the topping, add 2 tablespoons chopped walnuts to the apples
during cooking.

honey-pecan french toast with caramelized apples & pears
Prepare the basic recipe, adding 2 tablespoons honey to the custard. For
the topping, replace half the apples with pears.

variations

overnight caramel pecan french toast

see base recipe page 200

overnight caramel, raspberry & almond french toast
Prepare the basic recipe, replacing the pecans with almonds. Scatter
1/2 cup fresh raspberries on the first layer of bread in the dish, and
sprinkle 1 tablespoon sliced almonds over the top before chilling.
Garnish each serving with a few fresh raspberries.

overnight caramel, peach & pecan french toast
Prepare the basic recipe, scattering 1/2 cup peeled and chopped fresh peaches
on the first layer of bread in the dish. Add a few slices of peeled and sliced
fresh peaches to each serving.

overnight caramel, banana & walnut french toast
Prepare the basic recipe, replacing the pecans with walnuts. Add 2 sliced
bananas to the first layer of bread in the dish.

overnight caramel, chocolate & pecan french toast
Prepare the basic recipe, adding 1/2 cup chocolate chips to the first layer of
bread in the dish. Just before serving, sprinkle with grated semisweet chocolate.

big plates

Savor a long, chatty, weekend breakfast with big plates of eggs, meat, potatoes, and toast. Whatever your style, this chapter gives you abundant filling ideas to start your day.

kedgeree

see variations page 225

This is a traditional breakfast dish of Indian origin. It originally consisted of rice, onion, lentils, spices, fresh limes, butter, and fish.

butter, for greasing
2 hard-boiled eggs
1 lb. smoked fish, preferably haddock
4 cups boiled rice
1/4 tsp. ground nutmeg

2 tsp. freshly chopped parsley
salt and freshly ground black pepper
1/3 cup half-and-half
1/4 cup (1/2 stick) butter

Preheat the oven to 350°F and liberally butter a deep baking dish.

Cut the eggs into small wedges. Flake the fish into a medium bowl. Add the rice, nutmeg, and parsley, and season with salt and pepper. Pour in the half-and-half, add the eggs, and stir together lightly. Tip into the baking dish and dot with butter. Cover the dish with a lid and bake for about 30 minutes, until heated through. Serve immediately.

Serves 4

the great british fry-up

see variations page 226

This is an iconic breakfast, enjoyed by the British all around the world. Why not try making your own baked beans, using the smoky beans recipe on page 251.

vegetable oil, for cooking
8 pork sausages, the best you can buy (or make
    your own, recipe page 233)
8 rashers back bacon (or 12 strips bacon)
1 (16-oz.) can baked beans

2 cups sliced button mushrooms
4 ripe tomatoes, halved
toast or hash browns (see page 244), to serve
4 eggs

Heat the oven to 275°F. In a large skillet, heat a little vegetable oil. When it is hot, put in the sausages and cook them slowly, over a medium heat, for about 20 minutes until browned, turning them occasionally. Remove the sausages from the skillet and keep warm in the oven. Place the bacon in the skillet and fry for 2-4 minutes on each side until crisp and browned. Remove and keep warm in the oven. Heat baked beans slowly in a small saucepan while you cook the rest of the meal, stirring occasionally.

Increase the heat under the skillet and add the mushrooms. Cook, without stirring, for a few minutes, and when browned, remove from skillet and keep warm in the oven. Place tomatoes cut-side down in the skillet. Cook for 2 minutes on medium heat, gently turn over, and cook the other side for 2 minutes, until tender. Remove from skillet and keep warm in the oven. Prepare toast or warm hash-browns. The eggs are the last to cook and are best if served immediately. At this stage, place all the other ingredients onto serving plates and put back into the oven to keep warm.

Break an egg into a small bowl. Clean the skillet, add 3 or 4 tablespoons vegetable oil, and when it is hot, carefully tip in the egg. If the skillet is big enough, cook all 4 at once. Cook slowly, basting with the hot oil, until the white is cooked and the yolk is hot, or until it is cooked as you like it. You can flip it over if you prefer it over-easy. Once done, remove from the skillet immediately, add to the other items on the plates, and serve.

Serves 4

sausage & onion rosti

see variations page 227

This is an unusual way of serving rosti (a Swiss version of hash browns), with meaty sausages, browned and baked in the oven.

butter, for greasing
3 tbsp. olive oil
1 small onion, finely chopped
4 large peeled potatoes

8 sausages, the best you can buy, or make your own (page 233)
2 tbsp. freshly chopped parsley, to serve

Preheat the oven to 375°F and grease a nonstick 9x13-inch rectangular metal pan with butter. Heat 1 tablespoon olive oil in a small skillet, add the onion, and fry over medium heat for 6-8 minutes, until softened and lightly browned. Set aside.

Grate the potatoes into a sieve. Rinse with water, drain well, place in a dishtowel, and squeeze out as much water as possible. Spread the remaining oil in the roasting pan, add the potatoes, and bake for 10 minutes. Remove from the oven, scatter the onion on top, and place the sausages on top, evenly spaced. Bake for 20 minutes, then turn the sausages over.

Bake for 20 minutes more, or until the rosti is brown and crispy and so are the sausages. Serve immediately. Cut the rosti into fourths and place on serving plates, with 2 sausages each, and scatter the parsley over the top.

Serves 4

tex-mex sausage bake

see variations page 228

This will fill your kitchen with the wonderful aroma of cheese as it bakes in the oven. You can increase the "heat" of this dish by using jalapeño peppers and/or pepper jack cheese, if you wish.

1 lb. pork sausage, crumbled
6 scallions, chopped
1 red bell pepper, seeded and chopped
1/4 cup finely chopped mild green chiles
4 cups cooked 1/4-inch potato cubes
1 1/2 cups shredded Monterey Jack cheese

4 eggs
3/4 cup milk
salt and freshly ground black pepper
pinch cayenne pepper
few shakes of hot sauce
grated parmesan cheese, for sprinkling

Heat the oven to 350°F and grease a 2-quart rectangular baking dish. In a large skillet, cook the sausage for a few minutes until it starts to brown. Drain on paper towels. Put back into the skillet and add the scallions, pepper, and chiles. Fry until the sausage has cooked and the pepper has softened. In the baking dish, layer half the potatoes, half the cheese, and all the cooked sausage mixture. Top with the remaining potatoes and then the remaining cheese.

In a medium bowl, whisk the eggs and the milk together, then season with salt, pepper, cayenne pepper, and hot sauce to taste. Pour evenly over the mixture in the baking dish. Cover with a lid or foil that has been buttered so it does not stick. Bake for 60 minutes. Remove lid or foil, sprinkle top with Parmesan cheese, and bake for 10 minutes more, or until a knife inserted in the center comes out clean. Let it stand for 10 minutes before serving, cut into wedges.

Serves 6

corned beef hash with poached eggs

see variations page 229

I like this corned beef hash recipe because it's very well flavored. Try to keep the corned beef in chunks, rather than letting it cook down to a mash, so you can taste the different textures.

butter, for greasing
4 large potatoes, unpeeled, cut into cubes
3 tbsp. olive oil
1 onion, sliced
1 (12-oz.) can corned beef, cut into chunks
4 tbsp. Worcestershire sauce

1 large pickled gherkin, chopped
2 tsp. whole-grain mustard
salt and freshly ground black pepper
2 tbsp. freshly chopped parsley
4 poached eggs (see page 155), to serve

Preheat the broiler and grease a 2-quart baking dish generously with butter. In a large saucepan, boil the potato cubes for 5 minutes, then drain. In a large skillet, heat 2 tablespoons olive oil and fry the onion for a few minutes until softened and lightly browned. In a medium bowl, gently mix the corned beef chunks, onion, Worcestershire sauce, chopped gherkin, mustard, salt and pepper, and parsley.

In the skillet, heat the remaining oil, and fry the potatoes until they are tender and just starting to brown at the edges. Place the corned beef mixture in the baking dish and top with the potatoes. Place the dish under the broiler and broil until the top is crisp and golden brown, about 5-6 minutes. Serve immediately, topping each serving with a poached egg.

Serves 4

meat lovers' potato skillet

see variations page 230

If you'd like, you can cook the potatoes the night before, then cook this one-skillet meal in the morning. It's filling and satisfying. Serve it by itself or as a side dish for eggs.

3 cups 1/4-inch-cubed peeled potatoes
2 tbsp. vegetable oil, plus extra is required
1 medium onion, chopped
1/2 cup chopped spicy chorizo

1/2 cup chopped crisply cooked bacon
1/2 cup ham cut into strips
salt and freshly ground black pepper
2 tbsp. freshly chopped parsley, to serve

In a large saucepan, cook the cubed potatoes in boiling water for 5 minutes, then remove and drain well.

In a large skillet, heat 2 tablespoons vegetable oil over medium heat, then fry the onion for a few minutes until it has softened. Turn the heat to medium-high and add the potatoes to the skillet. Fry until they are crispy at the edges, adding more oil if necessary. Stir continuously until they are browned all over, then add all the meat. Season well with salt and pepper. Keep turning the mixture around the pan until the meat is heated through. Add chopped parsley and serve immediately.

Serves 4-5

ham, cheese & bacon tartiflette

see variations page 231

A tartiflette is a hot, bubbling dish with cheese and onion, originating in France. There, the cheese used is Reblochon, which may be difficult to find at the market.

1/4 cup (1/2 stick) unsalted butter, plus extra
    for greasing
2 1/2 lbs. potatoes, peeled and roughly chopped
1 onion, chopped
2 garlic cloves, finely chopped
1 tbsp. fresh thyme leaves

10 strips bacon, chopped
1/2 cup dry white wine
1 cup heavy cream
1/2 cup ham cut into strips
1 1/2 cups shredded Gruyère cheese
salt and freshly ground black pepper

Preheat the oven to 400°F, and grease a 2-quart baking dish generously with butter. In a large saucepan, boil the potatoes for 5 minutes, then drain. In a large skillet, melt the 1/4 cup butter over medium heat. Add the onion and fry for a few minutes until softened and lightly browned. Add the garlic, thyme, and chopped bacon, and cook for 5 minutes, stirring constantly. Stir in the wine, cream, ham, potatoes, and most of the cheese. Season with salt and pepper. Transfer to the baking dish and cover with a lid or foil that has been oiled to prevent it sticking. Bake for 20 minutes, then remove the lid or foil, sprinkle on the remaining cheese, and bake for 20 minutes more, or until bubbling and golden brown.

Serves 4

variations

kedgeree

see base recipe page 213

smoky kedgeree
Prepare the basic recipe, adding 2 teaspoons smoked paprika to the rice mixture.

kedgeree with bacon
Prepare the basic recipe, adding 1/4 cup cooked and crispy bacon to the
rice mixture.

kedgeree with mushrooms
Prepare the basic recipe, adding 1/4 cup cooked and sliced button mushrooms
to the rice mixture.

kedgeree with sausages
Prepare the basic recipe, adding 1/4 cup cooked and sliced sausage links to the
rice mixture.

kedgeree with a hint of curry
Prepare the basic recipe, adding 2 teaspoons curry powder to the rice mixture.

variations

the great british fry-up

see base recipe page 214

great british fry-up with fried bread
Prepare the basic recipe, replacing toast or hash browns with fried bread. To make it, quickly fry thick slices of white bread in very hot canola oil until crispy on both sides.

southern fry-up
Prepare the basic recipe, omitting the baked beans and the tomatoes. Replace with grits (cooked according to package directions) and fried green tomatoes, made by dipping unripened green tomato slices into cornmeal, seasoned with salt and pepper, and frying in a little oil or bacon fat.

vegetarian fry-up
Prepare the basic recipe, omitting all meat. Serve with a stuffed red bell pepper, made by cutting pepper in half lengthwise, and stuffing both halves with cooked rice mixed with chopped green onion and fresh parsley, and sprinkled with a little shredded Cheddar cheese. Bake on a greased pan for 15 minutes at 350°F.

pork chop fry-up
Prepare the basic recipe, replacing the sausages with a broiled or roasted pork chop.

variations

sausage & onion rosti

see base recipe page 217

sausage & onion rosti with bacon
Prepare the basic recipe, adding 1/4 cup chopped bacon to the skillet with the onion.

sausage & onion rosti with cheese
Prepare the basic recipe, sprinkling 1/2 cup shredded Cheddar cheese on top of the sausages and rosti 10 minutes before the end of cooking time.

sausage & onion rosti with mushrooms
Prepare the basic recipe, scattering 1/2 cup cooked and sliced button mushrooms on top of the sausages and rosti 10 minutes before the end of cooking time.

sausage & onion rosti with chile
Prepare the basic recipe, adding 1 finely chopped mild green chile to the skillet with the onion.

variations

tex-mex sausage bake

see base recipe page 218

tex-mex sausage bake with bacon
Prepare the basic recipe, adding 1/2 cup chopped bacon to the skillet with the onions.

tex-mex sausage bake with corn
Prepare the basic recipe, adding 1 (15-oz.) can whole kernel corn, drained, to the baking dish with the layers.

tex-mex sausage bake with mushrooms
Prepare the basic recipe, adding 1/2 cup sliced button mushrooms to the skillet with the onion.

tex-mex sausage bake with spicy chili beans
Prepare the basic recipe, adding1 (15-ounce) can spicy chili beans to the layers in the baking dish.

tex-mex sausage bake with corned beef
Prepare the basic recipe, replacing the sausage with corned beef.

corned beef hash with poached eggs

see base recipe page 220

corned beef hash with cheese & poached eggs
Prepare the basic recipe, sprinkling 1/2 cup shredded Cheddar cheese over the potatoes just before broiling.

corned beef hash with peppers & poached eggs
Prepare the basic recipe, adding 1 red bell pepper, seeded and sliced, to the skillet with the corned beef.

corned beef hash with mushrooms & poached eggs
Prepare the basic recipe, adding 1/2 cup sliced button mushrooms to the skillet with the onion.

corned beef hash with corn & poached eggs
Prepare the basic recipe, adding 1 (15-oz.) can whole kernel corn to the skillet with the corned beef.

corned beef hash with bacon & poached eggs
Prepare the basic recipe, sprinkling 1/4 cup cooked and crumbled crisp bacon over the potatoes and topping with 1/2 cup shredded Cheddar cheese just before broiling.

variations

meat lovers' potato skillet

see base recipe page 223

meat lovers' sweet potato skillet
Prepare the basic recipe, replacing half the potatoes with sweet potatoes.

meat lovers' potato & corn skillet
Prepare the basic recipe, adding 1 (15-ounce) can whole kernel corn, drained, to the skillet with the salt and pepper.

meat lovers' potato & chile skillet
Prepare the basic recipe, adding 1 mild green chile, finely chopped, to the skillet with the onion.

meat lovers' potato & tomato skillet
Prepare the basic recipe, adding 3 seeded and chopped tomatoes to the skillet with the salt and pepper.

meat lovers' potato & pepper skillet
Prepare the basic recipe, adding 1 green bell pepper, seeded and sliced, to the skillet with the onion.

variations

ham, cheese & bacon tartiflette

see base recipe page 224

ham, cheese & pancetta tartiflette
Prepare the basic recipe, replacing the bacon with chopped pancetta.

parma ham, cheese & bacon tartiflette
Prepare the basic recipe, replacing the ham with parma ham.

chorizo, cheese & bacon tartiflette
Prepare the basic recipe, replacing the ham with chopped chorizo.

ham, cheese, bacon & corn tartiflette
Prepare the basic recipe, adding 1 (15-ounce) can whole kernel corn, drained, to the skillet with the potatoes.

ham, cheese & bacon tartiflette with garlic
Prepare the basic recipe, adding 1 crushed garlic clove to the skillet with the onion.

sides &
sandwiches

When you're hosting a holiday brunch, you'll want

to include some of these hearty and delicious side

dishes. Sausages, glazed ham steak, oven-roasted

tomatoes, and hash browns will add the crowning

touch to your buffet table. Or grab a breakfast

calzone or burrito and dash off to work.

homemade pork sausages

see variations page 265

Making sausages is much easier than most people think. Sausage skins can quite often be purchased from butchers who make their own sausages. Alternatively, just roll into a sausage shape, and cut into sections about 4 or 5 inches in length. You could also form the sausage meat into patties and cook them like a burger, easy to put on a sausage sandwich. These can be frozen until needed; just defrost completely before cooking.

5 lbs. ground pork	1 tsp. ground mace
2 tsp. ground white pepper	3 tbsp. salt
1 tsp. ground ginger	2 cups fresh breadcrumbs
1 tsp. ground sage	hog casings, rinsed and drained on paper towels

In a large bowl, using your hands, combine all the ingredients (not the casings) together, making sure that the herbs and spices are distributed evenly.

If you have a sausage stuffer on a freestanding tabletop mixer, thread the hog casings onto the stuffer. You will find it easier to stuff the casings with two people, one to push the meat through and one to guide the casing off the stuffer, ensuring there is an even distribution of meat in the casing. This helps keep the sausages the same size. Keep going until you have used up all the meat. You can double the ingredients to make twice the number of sausages, if you can manage that amount. Twist sausages into links and store in refrigerator. Alternatively, after mixing the sausage, roll out on a floured work surface into a sausage shape and cut into sections about 4-5 inches in length. If not using immediately, store in the refrigerator.

Makes just over 5 pounds

gammon with pineapple salsa

see variations page 266

Gammon is a popular ham in England, and this recipe is gammon (ham steaks are a fine substitute) and pineapple with a twist. You can use fresh or canned pineapple for the salsa, but fresh is best.

for the pineapple salsa
2 tbsp. brown sugar
2 tbsp. soy sauce
2 cups finely chopped pineapple
    (preferably fresh)
1 red chile pepper, seeded and finely chopped
3 tbsp. freshly chopped cilantro

for the ham
2 large or 4 small thick ham steaks, rind on
2 tbsp. vegetable oil, for brushing and greasing
3 tsp. honey

First make the salsa. In a medium bowl, mix the soy sauce and the brown sugar together, and then add the rest of the ingredients. Mix well and set aside.

Preheat the broiler and grease a cookie sheet with a little oil. If you have large ham steaks, slice them in half so you have 4 portions. Carefully snip through the rind every 1/4 inch with scissors to prevent the steaks curling up during cooking. Brush the steaks with oil, and grill under the broiler for 3 or 4 minutes each side. Brush one side of each steak with honey and grill for another minute. Remove from the broiler and let stand for 3 minutes.

Serve with the salsa spooned on top of the ham steaks.

Serves 4

welsh rarebit

see variations page 267

This is sometimes mistakenly called Welsh rabbit. The success of this dish lies in cooking it slowly over a low heat until the cheese has melted.

2 cups good-quality shredded Cheddar cheese	3 tbsp. beer
2 tbsp. unsalted butter	salt and freshly ground black pepper to taste
1 tsp. dry mustard powder	4 slices buttered toast

Preheat the broiler. In a medium saucepan, cook the cheese, butter, mustard, and beer over a low heat. Season with salt and pepper. Stir occasionally until the mixture is smooth and creamy.

Spoon the cheese mix onto the toast, and put under the broiler to grill until golden and bubbling. Serve immediately.

Serves 4

potato hash bake

see variations page 268

This is delicious at a brunch buffet, and you can make it entirely in advance. Just reheat to serve.

2 tbsp. butter, plus extra for greasing
4 large potatoes, peeled and roughly diced
1 tbsp. olive oil
2 cups sliced button mushrooms
1 (15-oz.) can whole kernel corn, drained
4 tomatoes, quartered

1 small onion, finely chopped
6 scallions, chopped
3 tbsp. half-and-half
1 1/2 cups shredded Cheddar cheese
salt and freshly ground black pepper
3 tbsp. freshly chopped parsley, to garnish

Heat the oven to 350°F and generously grease a 2-quart baking dish with butter. In a large saucepan, boil the potatoes for 10-15 minutes until tender. Drain, tip back into the saucepan, and mash. In a medium saucepan, heat 1 tablespoon olive oil, add the mushrooms, and fry over medium heat for a few minutes until lightly browned and cooked through. Add the corn and tomatoes to the pan and stir together for a minute. Set aside.

In a medium skillet, melt the butter and fry the onion for a few minutes until softened and lightly browned. Tip into the mashed potatoes, with the butter from the pan, and add the chopped scallions. Mix well. Add half-and-half, and 1 cup of cheese. Season well with salt and freshly ground pepper. Place the mushrooms, corn, and tomatoes in the bottom of the baking dish, and spread the potato-onion mixture on top. Sprinkle the remaining cheese on top and bake in the oven for 20 minutes, or until the cheese has melted and the dish is a lovely golden brown. Serve immediately, sprinkled with a little freshly chopped parsley.

Serves 4

potato cakes with bacon & cheese

see variations page 269

These potato cakes make a delightful side dish, and are delicious served with smoky beans (page 251) and eggs.

2 lbs. potatoes
4 tbsp. butter
1 small onion, finely chopped
1 tsp. fresh thyme leaves
1/2 lb. green cabbage, finely sliced

2 tbsp. heavy cream
salt and freshly ground black pepper to taste
8 strips bacon
all-purpose flour, for dusting
4 slices Cheddar cheese

Peel the potatoes, and cut them into even-size chunks. Place them in a large saucepan, cover with water, and boil for about 20 minutes, until soft. Drain well and return to the pan. Put back over the heat for a minute, shaking slightly to make sure they are dry. Melt half the butter in another saucepan, and cook the chopped onion and thyme for about 5 or 6 minutes, until soft. Add the cabbage and a little water. Cover and cook until tender, then drain and add to the potatoes with the rest of the butter, the heavy cream, and plenty of salt and pepper. Mash the mixture well, divide into fourths, and shape into large potato cakes. Put on a greased cookie sheet and chill in the refrigerator for 1 hour.

Heat a large skillet, and fry the bacon until crisp. Remove bacon from pan and keep warm. Dust the potato cakes with flour and fry them in the bacon drippings for about 5 minutes each side, until crisp and golden. Top each cake with a slice of Cheddar cheese and transfer to a warmed plate. Place the bacon on top of each cake and serve immediately.

Makes 4

potato rosti

see variations page 270

Unlike the sausage & rosti recipe in the last chapter, this rosti uses shredded boiled potatoes before being made into a cake shape and baked in the oven. I find oven-baking rosti much easier and quicker than frying it on the stove.

butter, for greasing and for cooking
6 strips bacon
3 lbs. russet potatoes, peeled

6 tbsp. olive oil
1 medium onion, minced and drained
of moisture

Heat the oven to 375°F and generously butter an 8-inch cake pan with butter. Put a cookie sheet in the oven to heat.

In a large skillet, fry the bacon until golden and crisp, remove, and drain on paper towels. Break into small pieces.

In a large saucepan, boil the whole potatoes for 5 minutes, drain, and drop into iced water. When cold enough to handle, shred the potatoes into a large bowl. Mix in oil gradually, then add the drained onion and bacon pieces. Tip the potato mixture into the cake pan, do not press it down, and dot with butter over the top. Place the pan on the hot cookie sheet in the oven and bake for 1 hour 20 minutes, until the potatoes are cooked through and crispy on top. Serve immediately, cut into wedges, like slices of cake.

Serves 6-8

hash browns

see variations page 271

These are very similar to rosti, but they're the American version of the Swiss classic. They take a little planning, as you start them the night before.

8 large russet potatoes, peeled   1 tsp. freshly ground black pepper
2 tsp. salt   4 tbsp. butter with a little vegetable oil added

In a large saucepan, boil the whole potatoes for 15-20 minutes, until just tender. Drain, pat dry, and chill in the refrigerator overnight.

The next morning, shred the potatoes into a large bowl, and add the salt and pepper. Heat the butter and vegetable oil in a large skillet. Add the potatoes and cook for 8-10 minutes, or until golden brown on the bottom. Tip out onto a plate, then slide back into the pan to cook the other side. Cook until golden brown and crispy underneath, about 8-10 minutes. Serve immediately.

Serves 8

chili cheese breakfast casserole

see variations page 272

There are so many breakfast recipes with potatoes or bread that rice makes a welcome change. Try serving this the next time you have a brunch buffet.

butter, for greasing
1 cup uncooked long-grain white rice
2 cups water
1 cup cottage cheese
1 (15-oz.) can whole kernel corn, drained

1 red bell pepper, finely chopped
1 green bell pepper, finely chopped
1 cup sour cream
1/4 cup finely chopped mild green chiles
1 cup shredded Monterey Jack cheese

Heat the oven to 350°F and grease a 2-quart baking dish with butter.

In a large saucepan, cook the rice in the water, as directed on the package, usually 10 minutes until all the water is absorbed. Place the rice in a bowl to cool slightly. Add the cottage cheese, corn, red and green peppers, sour cream, and chiles. Mix well. Put the mixture into the baking dish and sprinkle the cheese over the top. Bake for 30-35 minutes, until thoroughly heated and the cheese has melted. Serve immediately.

Serves 6

wild rice cakes

see variations page 273

These rice cakes are not commonly seen as a breakfast item, but if you are trying to lower your carbohydrate intake, they make a spicy alternative to hash browns. Wear rubber gloves when chopping chiles, because they can irritate your skin.

1/3 cup uncooked wild rice
2 cups water
1 tbsp. flour
1 tsp. baking powder
1/2 tsp. salt

1 mild green chile, finely chopped
3 tbsp. minced onion
1 egg
1 tbsp. finely chopped and peeled fresh ginger
2 tbsp. olive oil

In a medium saucepan, boil the rice in 2 cups water for about 40 minutes, until tender. Drain and place in a bowl. Sprinkle the flour, baking powder, and salt over the rice, and stir until combined.

In a small bowl, whisk together the chile, onion, egg, and ginger, and add to the rice mixture.

In a large skillet, heat the oil over medium heat. Put 2 tablespoons rice mixture into the pan and shape to form cakes. Cook 4 at a time for 3 minutes on each side, until golden brown. Drain on paper towels. Keep warm while you make the rest. Serve immediately.

Makes 8 cakes

smoky beans with bacon & basil

see variations page 274

Homemade baked beans, served as a delicious accompaniment to eggs or sausages, or as a topping for toast, for a perfect start to the day.

2 tbsp. olive oil
1 large onion, finely chopped
1 tsp. smoked paprika
2 (15-oz.) cans cannellini beans, drained
5 large fresh tomatoes, seeded and chopped

8 strips bacon
large handful fresh basil leaves
salt and freshly ground black pepper
few shakes of hot sauce

In a medium saucepan, heat the oil and add the onion. Cook over high heat for about 5 minutes until softened and starting to brown. Turn the heat down a little, add the paprika, drained beans, and chopped tomatoes to the pan and cook for a few minutes.

In a large skillet, fry the bacon until crisp and golden, then break into bite-size pieces. Set aside.

Shred the basil and add to the pan with the salt and freshly ground black pepper. Add a few shakes of hot sauce. Continue to cook until the tomatoes have broken down a little and the basil has wilted. Serve immediately, with the bacon sprinkled over the top.

Serves 4

bacon-wrapped portobello mushrooms

see variations page 275

You cook these mushrooms in the oven, but you can also grill them under the broiler or on the outside grill. They're great with scrambled eggs and sausages or as part of a breakfast buffet. You could also serve them on toast.

2 tsp. vegetable oil, for brushing and greasing
8 large portobello mushrooms
8 strips bacon

Preheat the oven to 375°F or preheat the broiler. Grease a cookie sheet with vegetable oil. Wipe the mushrooms clean, and wrap each one with a bacon strip. Place on the cookie sheet and brush lightly with a little vegetable oil. Place in the oven and bake for 10 minutes, until the bacon is crispy. Alternatively, cook under the broiler, watching carefully to make sure the bacon does not burn. Serve immediately.

Serves 8

oven-roasted vine tomatoes

see variations page 276

These are so simple to do, and tomatoes take on a completely different flavor when oven-roasted with olive oil. Leaving them on the vine makes them look special.

olive oil for brushing and greasing
16-20 small tomatoes on the vine

3 tsp. fresh thyme leaves
salt and freshly ground black pepper to taste

Preheat the oven to 375°F and grease a cookie sheet with olive oil.

Keeping the tomatoes on the vine, snip them into groups of 4 or 5. Place on the cookie sheet, brush the tomatoes carefully with olive oil, and sprinkle the thyme leaves and salt and pepper over them. Bake in the oven for 15-20 minutes, until the tomatoes have softened. Serve immediately.

Serves 4

breakfast wraps

see variations page 277

Wrap up your scrambled eggs in a flour tortilla to take with you to eat on the way to work or school. Tortillas come in different sizes, so you can make your sandwich any size you want.

2 tsp. vegetable oil
3 eggs
salt and freshly ground black pepper
1/2 cup chopped ham

2 tbsp. finely chopped green bell pepper
3 tbsp. shredded Cheddar cheese
2 flour tortillas

In a large skillet, heat a little vegetable oil. In a medium bowl, whisk the eggs, season with salt and pepper to taste, and stir in the ham and green bell pepper. Pour into the skillet and stir with a wooden spoon to scramble the eggs. Cook until almost set, add the cheese, and cook for another minute or until the cheese is melted.

Heat the tortillas by steaming them in the microwave in moist paper towels (or use a tortilla steamer) for 30 seconds. Spoon the filling into the middle of each tortilla. Roll up and serve immediately.

Serves 2

breakfast sausage burger with bacon & cheese

see variations page 278

Very similar to fast food, but much better homemade.

1 lb. pork sausage
1 tbsp. fresh thyme leaves
2 tsp. freshly ground black pepper
2 tbsp. vegetable oil

8 strips bacon
4 slices cheese
4 hamburger buns, split

Preheat the broiler and preheat the oven to 325°F. Put 4 serving plates in the oven to warm. In a large bowl, mix the sausage with the thyme leaves and black pepper. Form into 4 patties. In a large skillet, heat the oil, and fry the patties for a few minutes until golden brown and cooked through. Drain on paper towels.

Put the bacon in the skillet and fry for a few minutes until crisp and cooked through. Remove and drain on paper towels. Place the hamburger halves on a cookie sheet and broil until golden brown.

Assemble the burgers. Put the bottom half of the buns on warm serving plates. Put a sausage patty on each bun and top with a slice of cheese and 2 strips of bacon placed across the cheese. Put the top half of the buns on top and put the plates back in the oven for 3 minutes to heat through and to slightly melt the cheese. Serve immediately.

Serves 4

bacon sandwich with apple & blue cheese

see variations page 279

Is there anything more evocative of lazy weekend mornings than the scent of frying bacon? Here is a bacon sandwich with a twist—the flavors go really well together, and create a satisfying sandwich that will fill you up all morning.

2 tsp. vegetable oil
10 strips bacon (or 6 rashers back bacon)
1 apple, peeled, cored, and sliced

4 thick slices white bread
butter, for spreading
1/4 cup Stilton or other blue cheese

In a large skillet, melt the oil and fry the bacon over medium heat for about 3-4 minutes each side, until crisp and golden. Add the apple slices to the pan and sauté over a medium heat for 3 minutes, or until golden and tender. Remove from heat.

Spread the bread with butter, and divide the bacon and apple between two slices. Crumble the blue cheese over the top, and place the other 2 slices of bread on top. Serve immediately.

Serves 2

mini breakfast calzones

see variations page 280

Mini calzones are delicious, filling, and easily portable if needed.

for the dough
1 tsp. sugar
1 1/4 cups warm water (110°F)
1 envelope dry yeast
4 cups white bread flour
1 level tsp. salt
1 tbsp. olive oil

for the filling
2 tsp. vegetable oil
1 lb. pork sausage, crumbled
1 small onion, chopped
2 tsp. dried basil
2 tsp. dried oregano
1/4 cup tomato pizza sauce

Prepare the yeast liquid by dissolving the sugar in the warm water. Sprinkle the yeast on top and leave until frothy, about 10 minutes. Sift the flour and salt into a large bowl, make a well in the center, and add the yeast liquid and olive oil together. Work to a firm dough, turn onto a lightly floured surface, and knead thoroughly with your hands and knuckles until you have a soft, smooth, and elastic dough. Alternatively, knead the dough in a freestanding tabletop mixer for 5 minutes. Put the dough into a greased bowl, turning to coat it all over, and cover with plastic wrap. Let rise in a warm place until doubled in size.

While the dough is rising, make the filling. In a large skillet, heat a little oil, add the crumbled sausage, and cook until it is no longer pink. Add the chopped onion and fry for a few minutes until the mixture is cooked and browned. Add the basil, oregano, and pizza sauce. Stir to mix well and set aside to cool completely.

Turn the dough onto a lightly floured surface and knock back slightly. Divide into 18 pieces, shaping into balls. Roll out the balls to a 6-inch circle and place 1 tablespoon filling in the middle. Slightly wet the edges and gather the edges together at the top to enclose the filling. Turn the rolls upside down and roll out slightly, pressing them down gently without forcing the filling out. Place on floured cookie sheets, with the seam underneath, dust with flour, cover loosely, and let rise until doubled in size. Heat the oven to 425°F. Remove the covering and bake the rolls for 15-20 minutes. Remove from the oven and cool slightly on a wire rack.

Makes 18

breakfast burritos

see variations page 281

Ready for breakfast Tex-Mex style?

2 tsp. vegetable oil
6 oz. pork breakfast sausage
2 tbsp. finely chopped onion
1 tbsp. finely chopped mild or hot green chile
4 eggs, beaten

salt and freshly ground black pepper
4 large (10-inch) tortillas
4 slices American cheese
salsa and guacamole, to serve

Heat oil in a skillet over medium heat, then crumble the sausage into the pan. Add the onion. Cook for 5 minutes until the sausage is browned and the onion is softened and lightly colored. Add the chopped chile, stir for another minute, and then add the beaten eggs. Scramble using a wooden spoon until the eggs begin to set. Season with salt and pepper and remove from heat.

Heat the tortillas either by steaming in the microwave in moist paper towels, or in a tortilla steamer, for 30 seconds. Break each slice of cheese in half and place end to end in the middle of each tortilla. Spoon a quarter of the egg filling on top of the cheese on each of the tortillas. Fold one side of each tortilla over the filling, then fold up about 2 inches of one end. Fold over the other side of the tortilla to complete the burritos, leaving one end open. Serve immediately, with a little salsa and guacamole on the side.

Serves 4

variations

pork sausages

see base recipe page 233

lincolnshire sausages
Prepare the basic recipe, adding 1 tablespoon freshly chopped parsley,
1 tablespoon freshly chopped sage, and 1 tablespoon fresh thyme leaves to
the mixture.

cumberland sausages
Prepare the basic recipe, adding 1 tablespoon freshly ground black pepper
to the mixture, and when shaping the sausage, make it in to a long
circular spiral.

pork & leek sausages
Prepare the basic recipe, adding 1 cup cooked, well-drained, and finely chopped
leeks to the mixture.

spicy peri-peri sausages
Prepare the basic recipe, adding 1/2 teaspoon peri-peri sauce to the mixture.
Adjust the amount to your own personal taste.

pork & apple sausages
Prepare the basic recipe, adding 2 peeled, cored, and chopped Granny Smith
apples to the meat mixture.

variations

gammon with pineapple salsa

see base recipe page 234

gammon with pineapple & red pepper salsa
Prepare the basic recipe, adding 1 teaspoon crushed red pepper flakes to
the salsa.

orange-glazed gammon with pineapple salsa
Prepare the basic recipe, replacing the honey with orange marmalade.

gammon with pineapple & pear salsa
Prepare the basic recipe, adding 1 pear, peeled, cored and chopped, to
the salsa.

mustard-glazed gammon & poached eggs
Prepare the basic recipe, replacing the honey with honey mustard. Instead of
serving with salsa, serve with poached eggs (page 155).

cider-marinated gammon with pineapple salsa
Prepare the basic recipe, but marinate the gammon in a little apple cider for
an hour before cooking.

variations

welsh rarebit

see base recipe page 237

welsh rarebit with worcestershire sauce
Prepare the basic recipe, adding 2 teaspoons Worcestershire sauce to
the cheese.

welsh rarebit with poached eggs
Prepare the basic recipe, and add a poached egg (page 155) on top of the
rarebit, just before serving.

welsh rarebit with herbs
Prepare the basic recipe, adding 1 tablespoon freshly chopped mixed herbs to
the cheese.

variations

potato hash bake

see base recipe page 238

potato hash bake with bacon
Prepare the basic recipe, adding 1/2 cup chopped bacon to the pan with the mushrooms, and sauté until crisp.

potato hash bake with swiss cheese
Prepare the basic recipe, replacing the Cheddar cheese with Gruyère cheese.

potato hash bake with pancetta
Prepare the basic recipe, adding 1/2 cup chopped pancetta to the pan with the mushrooms.

potato hash bake with asparagus
Prepare the basic recipe, adding a few spears of steamed asparagus to the vegetables in the bottom of the baking dish.

potato hash bake with salmon
Prepare the basic recipe, adding 1 lightly poached salmon fillet to the pan with the vegetables.

variations

potato cakes with bacon & cheese

see base recipe page 240

potato cakes with cod & parsley
Prepare the basic recipe, omitting the cabbage and thyme, and replacing them with
3/4 pound cooked, boneless, flaked cod, and freshly chopped parsley. Top with the
cheese and bacon, if desired.

salmon potato cakes
Prepare the basic recipe, omitting the cabbage and thyme, and substituting with
3/4 pound of boneless, flaked salmon fillet, and freshly chopped parsley. Top with
the cheese and bacon, if desired.

potato cakes with bacon & swiss cheese
Prepare the basic recipe, replacing the Cheddar cheese with sliced Swiss cheese.

spicy potato cakes
Prepare the basic recipe, adding 2 teaspoons crushed red chile pepper flakes to the
potato mixture.

potato cakes with crab
Prepare the basic recipe, replacing the cabbage with 3/4 pound cooked, canned or
fresh, boneless, flaked crabmeat. Top with the cheese and bacon, if desired.

variations

potato rosti

see base recipe page 243

italian potato rosti
Prepare the basic recipe, adding 3 teaspoons dried Italian herbs to the skillet
with the onion.

mexican potato rosti
Prepare the basic recipe, adding 1 tablespoon crushed dried red pepper
flakes to the skillet with the onion.

potato rosti with pancetta
Prepare the basic recipe, adding 1/4 cup chopped pancetta to the skillet with
the onion.

french potato rosti
Prepare the basic recipe, adding 1 crushed clove of garlic to the skillet with
the onion.

potato & parsnip rosti
Prepare the basic recipe, replacing a third of the potato with parsnips.

variations

hash browns

see base recipe page 244

spicy hash browns
Prepare the basic recipe, adding 1 teaspoon Cajun seasoning and
1/4 teaspoon cayenne pepper to the potatoes with the salt and pepper.

hash browns with cheese
Prepare the basic recipe. Ten minutes before the end of cooking, sprinkle
1/2 cup shredded Cheddar cheese over the potatoes.

hash browns with bacon
Prepare the basic recipe, adding 5 strips of bacon, cooked until crisp, and
crumbled, to the potatoes with the salt and pepper.

hash browns with chile
Prepare the basic recipe, adding 2 teaspoons dried crushed red chile flakes
to the potatoes with the salt and pepper.

red flannel hash
Prepare the basic recipe, adding 1 boiled and shredded beet to the potatoes
with the salt and pepper.

variations

chili cheese breakfast casserole

see base recipe page 247

chili cheese & bacon breakfast casserole
Prepare the basic recipe, adding 1/2 cup cooked and crispy bacon.

chili cheese & tomato breakfast casserole
Prepare the basic recipe, adding 2 seeded and chopped tomatoes.

chili swiss cheese breakfast casserole
Prepare the basic recipe, replacing the Monterey Jack cheese with Gruyère cheese.

chili cheese & parma breakfast casserole
Prepare the basic recipe, adding 1/2 cup chopped Parma ham.

chili cheese & chorizo breakfast casserole
Prepare the basic recipe, replacing the cheese with pepperjack cheese. Add a few jalapeños and 1/4 cup chopped chorizo.

variations

wild rice cakes

see base recipe page 248

smoky wild rice & bulgur wheat cakes with smoked salmon
Prepare the basic recipe, replacing half the wild rice with 1/3 cup cooked bulgur wheat. Add 2 teaspoons smoked paprika to the rice mixture. Top with a thin slice of smoked salmon and serve accompanied by a slice of fresh lemon.

wild rice cakes with tomato
Prepare the basic recipe, adding 1 seeded and chopped tomato to the rice mixture.

rice cakes with wild mushrooms
Prepare the basic recipe, replacing half the wild rice with 1/3 cup cooked brown rice. Add 1/4 cup very finely chopped wild mushrooms to the rice mixture.

wild rice cakes with cheese & chives
Prepare the basic recipe, adding 1/2 cup shredded Cheddar cheese and 2 tablespoons freshly chopped chives to the rice mixture.

wild rice cakes with poached egg & herbs
Prepare the basic recipe, and add 2 tablespoons crushed mixed herbs to the rice mixture. Serve topped with poached eggs (page 155).

variations

smoky beans with bacon & basil

see base recipe page 251

quick smoky beans with apple
Instead of the basic recipe, in a 2-quart baking dish, mix together
2 (16-ounce) cans Boston baked beans, 1 peeled and chopped Granny Smith
apple, 1 tablespoon Dijon mustard, 4 tablespoons ketchup, 1 tablespoon
Worcestershire sauce, and 1/4 cup brown sugar. Heat until just simmering,
then bake at 350°F for 25 minutes until the apple is tender. Serve
immediately, with crisp, crumbled bacon sprinkled on top.

smoky beans with celery, chorizo & basil
Prepare the basic recipe, replacing the bacon with 1/2 cup chopped chorizo.
Add 1/2 cup chopped celery with the chopped tomatoes.

smoky black beans with bacon, peppers & basil
Prepare the basic recipe, replacing the cannellini beans with canned black
beans. Add 1 chopped green bell pepper to the skillet and cook with the
onion until tender.

smoky beans with parma ham & cilantro
Prepare the basic recipe, replacing the bacon with Parma ham and the basil
with cilantro.

variations

bacon-wrapped portobello mushrooms

see base recipe page 252

herbed bacon-wrapped portobellos
Prepare the basic recipe, and sprinkle 2 tablespoons chopped mixed fresh herbs over the mushrooms before cooking.

cajun-spiced bacon-wrapped portobellos
Prepare the basic recipe, and sprinkle 1 tablespoon Cajun seasoning over the mushrooms before cooking.

sweet & spicy bacon-wrapped portobellos
Prepare the basic recipe, sprinkling the mushrooms before cooking with a mixture of 1 tablespoon brown sugar and 1 teaspoon mild chili powder.

bacon-wrapped portobellos with cheese
Prepare the basic recipe, and sprinkle on a little finely grated Parmesan cheese before cooking.

pancetta-wrapped portobellos
Prepare the basic recipe, replacing the bacon with pancetta.

variations

oven-roasted vine tomatoes

see base recipe page 254

oven-roasted vine tomatoes with garlic
Prepare the basic recipe, adding 1 crushed garlic clove to the thyme before sprinkling it over the tomatoes.

oven-roasted vine tomatoes with walnuts
Prepare the basic recipe, brushing the tomatoes with walnut oil instead of olive oil and adding 2 tablespoons finely chopped walnuts to the thyme before sprinkling it over the tomatoes.

oven-roasted vine tomatoes with oregano & basil
Prepare the basic recipe, replacing the fresh thyme leaves with freshly chopped oregano and basil.

oven-roasted vine tomatoes with pesto
Prepare the basic recipe, omitting the fresh thyme leaves. Instead of brushing tomatoes with olive oil, brush them with 4 teaspoons pesto.

oven-roasted vine tomatoes with parmesan cheese
Prepare the basic recipe, adding a sprinkling of Parmesan cheese on the tomatoes 10 minutes before the end of cooking time.

breakfast wraps

see base recipe page 257

breakfast wraps with tomato
Prepare the basic recipe, adding 3 tomatoes, seeded and chopped, to the filling.

breakfast wraps with feta cheese
Prepare the basic recipe, adding 1/4 cup feta cheese to the filling.

breakfast wraps with feta, olives & mint
Prepare the basic recipe, omitting the Cheddar cheese and substituting 1/4 cup feta cheese, 2 tablespoons pitted and chopped black olives, and 1 tablespoon freshly chopped mint to the filling.

breakfast wraps with bacon
Prepare the basic recipe, adding 4 strips of bacon, cooked until crispy and broken into small pieces, to the filling.

breakfast wraps with chiles
Prepare the basic recipe, adding 2 tablespoons chopped, canned jalapeño peppers to the filling.

variations

breakfast sausage burger with bacon & cheese

see base recipe page 258

spicy sausage burger with bacon & cheese
Prepare the basic recipe, adding 1 teaspoon ground cumin to the
sausage mixture.

hot sausage burger with bacon & cheese
Prepare the basic recipe, adding half a chopped hot green chile to the
sausage during mixing.

italian sausage burger with bacon & cheese
Prepare the basic recipe, replacing the thyme leaves in the sausage mixture
with 2 teaspoons dried oregano and 2 teaspoons dried basil.

egg sausage burger on sourdough
Prepare the basic recipe, replacing the hamburger buns with 8 slices of
sourdough bread. Add a poached or fried egg on top of the sausage on
each burger.

breakfast sausage & onion burger with bacon & cheese
Prepare the basic recipe, adding 4 scallions, finely chopped, to the
sausage mixture.

bacon sandwich with apple & blue cheese

see base recipe page 261

bacon sandwich with fried egg & brown sauce
Make the variation above, adding a fried egg to each sandwich. Add
1–2 teaspoons brown sauce to each sandwich.

bacon sandwich with apple & cheddar
Prepare the basic recipe, replacing the blue cheese with shredded
Cheddar cheese.

bacon sandwich with pear & blue cheese
Prepare the basic recipe, replacing the apple with a pear.

bacon sandwich with apple & dill pickle
Prepare the basic recipe, replacing the blue cheese with a few slices of
dill pickle.

bacon sandwich with tomato & tomato chutney
Prepare the basic recipe, omitting the apple and blue cheese and
substituting a few slices of tomato and 2–3 teaspoons tomato chutney
on each sandwich.

variations

mini breakfast calzones

see base recipe page 262

quick mini breakfast calzones

Prepare the basic recipe, but instead of making the dough, use purchased 1-pound refrigerated pizza dough.

mini breakfast calzones with chorizo

Prepare the basic recipe, replacing the sausage with finely chopped chorizo.

mini breakfast calzones with eggs

Prepare the basic recipe, adding 2 chopped hard-boiled eggs to the filling.

mini breakfast calzones with sausage & eggs

Prepare the basic recipe, but use purchased pizza dough rolled into 6-inch circles. Omit onion, herbs, and pizza sauce. Cook sausage and sprinkle onto pizza circle. Top with well-seasoned, lightly scrambled eggs and slices of your favorite cheese. Fold over half the dough, seal edges, and bake at 425°F for about 15–20 minutes.

mini breakfast calzones with sun-dried tomatoes

Prepare the basic recipe, adding 1/4 cup chopped sun-dried tomatoes to the filling.

variations

breakfast burritos

see base recipe page 264

breakfast burritos with refried beans

Prepare the basic recipe, omitting the filling. Make a filling from 1/4 cup refried beans, crumbled crisp bacon, a little arugula, and 1/4 cup shredded Monterey Jack cheese. Spoon salsa on top of the filling before rolling.

egg-wrapped breakfast burritos

Prepare the basic recipe, omitting the flour tortillas. Make the wraps out of omelets. For each wrap, use 1 egg, swirled around in the skillet to make it as thin as possible.

egg-wrapped vegetarian breakfast burrito

Use the egg wrap from the variation above. Use the refried bean filling, without the bacon, from the refried bean variation.

breakfast burritos with ham & swiss

Prepare the basic recipe, omitting the sausage and its cooking step and substituting 1/3 cup chopped ham. Replace the American cheese with Swiss cheese.

index